More praise for

When I Do Relationsl
How Do They Go *So*
by Dana Elken Terrell

Books on improving relationships abound but few have the depth of consistent wisdom that is found on the pages of this book. Dana Terrell has achieved this through her applied knowledge of Bowen theory. She has made this theory her own with her unique integration of EMDR. This makes for a valuable book for anyone who cares about their relationship health—and let's face it, there is no way to improved well-being without finding ways to do our relationships better.

> Jenny Brown, PhD, author of the excellent self-help book based on Bowen theory: *Growing Yourself Up: How to bring your best to all of life's relationships*

. . . .

From desensitization to discovery: merging two unlikely psychotherapies: Not only has Dana Terrell found the nexus that connects EMDR with Bowen family systems therapy, she offers a delicious rendering of both approaches along with poignant time capsules of her own life, enticing case examples, and "relationship ouches" as entre points into individual work. Bowen has been one of my inner guides since reading an anthology of his papers in my twenties. Thank you, Dana, for bringing him back to life for a new generation of psychotherapists and seekers of personal growth.

> Kate Cohen-Posey, MS, LMHC, LMFT
> *Making Hostile Words Harmless*

. . . .

This book touched my heart and life on so many levels. I'm glad Dana explained her view that panic comes from untreated PTSD. It was true for me. I suffered with panic attacks for years. No one understood that it was from months in a hospital so far from home in a ward with very handicapped children, in a body cast strapped in a bed.

I am so thankful Dana Terrell was courageous enough to study and apply these beautiful principles to herself and came to understand human fears, behaviors, and patterns in order to teach the world. Otherwise, she could have become very "frozen" like her dear mother.

I found the section on caregiving and care-receiving valuable. It is crucial for critically ill people to feel supported and loved. This is foundational to healing the immune system.

Ellen Tart-Jensen,
Health Is Your Birthright

. . . .

I give permission to include my Dad's story in your book. What you are doing is very good. It will help a lot of people.

Ronald Medicine Crow, son of Chief Joe Medicine Crow

. . . .

Endorsement from a reader prior to publication: After reading your book, I woke up at 3 a.m. with many thoughts, one of which was that everything would be OK in my relationship with my 32-year old daughter. She never seemed to grow out of the teenage condescending attitude towards parents. Now that she's a surgical resident working 80+ hours a week, two things are working against us: one up/one down reciprocity (inherent in people with medical degrees?) and emotional-cutoff (due to her demanding schedule).

Yet I now have a sense that everything will be fine, remembering how deep our preteen connection was, and even have ideas on how to rekindle that. I can't tell you how astounding this is for me. I have a date to meet two friends as we are all troubled by our strained/estranged relationships with our adult children. I attribute my new hope to the Bowen material in this book.

Shared anonymously

When I Do Relationships *SO RIGHT* How Do They Go *SO WRONG*

Find inner strength

by calm, courageous, daily practice

of your most beloved principles.

Your character will shine,

and light the generations to come.

Dana Elken Terrell

When I Do Relationships
SO RIGHT
How Do They Go
SO WRONG

USING EMOTIONAL MATURITY
To Transform Your *MIND*, Your *RELATIONSHIPS*,
and the *GENERATIONS TO COME*

Dana Elken Terrell

Written by: Dana Elken Terrell, LCSW, EAC (LCS 13773)

Published by:
Comprehensive Therapy Approach, Inc.
3537 Boundary Street, San Diego, CA 92104
619 283-5665
www.iBEtherapy.com
connect@iBEtherapy.com

This book is accurate to the themes that universally affect humankind. But all names and identifying characteristics of individuals who have shared their stories have been changed, when requested, to protect their privacy.

Cover design: Michael James Canales
Interior graphics: Austin C. Donnell
Editors: Jan Tucker, Debbie Rosenblatt
Proofreader: Maggie Edwards

First Edition, Second printing, May 2018

ISBN: paperback: 978-1-948711-01-2
         hardcover: 978-1-948711-00-5
E-ISBN: 978-1-948711-02-9
Audiobook ISBN: 13:978-1-948711-03-6
Library of Congress Control Number: 2018901785

Printed in the United States

Dedicated with love

To my dear, departed parents, Lucille Evanson Elken and
Richard Guy Elken,
For their noble examples of loving commitment to one another and
to all they loved, for their positive outlook, doing their best
and for Dad's believing in me as a writer and
encouraging me to write a book.
I gave him one of the first drafts shortly before his passing in 2012.

And to my dear husband, David Loren Terrell (1951 to 2017),
For his sweet love and joy, his commitment to the love
and practice of high principles,
and for finding countless ways to support my purpose:
to serve the cause of greater emotional maturity.
He called this "our book."

David was a great believer in EMDR therapy and Bowen theory. He served at my June 2017 workshop as the "emotional protection team member." When he introduced himself, he shared how many EMDR sessions he experienced. Thus, he set a great example that it is ok to get your needs met and heal. He overcame more significant difficulties (alcoholism, anxiety, and cancer) than anyone I know personally (I'm not speaking clinically now).

I say he overcame cancer because he often said cancer was the best thing that ever happened to him. He sincerely meant it. For one thing, he never knew how much he was loved till his diagnosis. In his last months, he was in a beautiful state of loving everyone and everything. For another thing, once he got on disability, he used his free time for spiritual effort and was filled with joy and bliss much of the time. So, it was a true statement. With his super positive attitude, he turned it into a total blessing.

When he introduced me at the workshop, he claimed that I was a "world famous EMDR therapist." Feeling embarrassed, I didn't want to contradict him, so I simply hinted at his bias by saying, "he is my greatest fan." The group erupted in applause.

Table of Contents

Acknowledgments

I am grateful to so many people, and unfortunately do not have space here to name you all or to express my gratitude completely. I wish to thank:

Francine Shapiro, PhD for being the perfect person to discover EMDR. She has inspired, encouraged, and cajoled scientists and therapists to research EMDR further. Shapiro founded EMDR Humanitarian Assistance Program (now the Trauma Recovery Network, or TRN) in response to the bombing of the World Trade Center in 1993.

Ignacio Jarero, PhD and Lucy Artigas, MA of Mexico for their prayer in 1997 that led to the invention of the butterfly hug and a group EMDR protocol I adapted for iBE therapy.

Murray Bowen, MD whose patient development of family systems theory made a major difference in my life and that of so many others. Thanks to my coaches: Mary Bourne, LCSW, Laura Havstad, PhD; Carolyn Jacobs, PsyD, Michael Kerr, MD, and Roberta Gilbert, MD.

My clients who have opened their lives to me, to Bowen, and EMDR, and faced their difficulties. Many have let me share their stories as a help to others.

My friends of nearly forty years: Debbie Rosenblatt, Lauretta Daines, Cheryl Woodard, and Leslie King have attended my workshops and contributed suggestions, editing, and stories.

Jan Tucker, whose developmental editing has been spot on. Her writing expertise, and marketing and publishing knowledge made her the perfect editor. Maggie Edwards' proofreading was wonderful.

Richard Simon Kahn has been my book mentor, giving detailed feedback on title ideas, the book cover, and many practical matters outside of my expertise.

My writers group, including leader Mark Carstersen, Sara Sheen, Aura Hill, Kara Sjoblom-Bay, Matthew Portman, Adam, Suhan, David Barnes, Aura, Julia, and Sherman Cho. But for them and the help of Camp Nanowrimo and the National Novel Writer's Month, this book may not exist.

Patti Sandoval and Gloria Green for hosting book-signing parties. Their encouragement, cheerleading and joy have meant so much.

My EMDR colleagues and mentors, including the late Liz Snyker, LCSW whom we affectionately called the Mother of EMDR. My dear colleagues have given inspiration and example which have encouraged me to thrive.

Bernadette Talia, LCSW and Janet Sobel, Esq. have weekly served in our mastermind group since 2009.

The support of family and friends have meant so much: my late husband and late parents, my children Jacob and Lauren, Aunt Fran Evanson, and mother-in-law Beverly Terrell and all else I would love to mention by name. You know who you are. The strengths of principle, integrity, prayer, love, and joy you practice are treasures held in my heart.

A special thanks to those who have hosted and participated in iBE workshops in their areas.

Alexis Asquith and Kirk Hensler for their video-recording and web work.

I thank you all from my heart. Your love and countless, unique ways to contribute are woven into the book, the workshop, and all my future endeavors to sincerely serve the greater good.

Introduction

Human beings are social creatures. We develop many relationships throughout our lives. These relationships are critically important for our survival. Our family, friends, and others in our social network sustain us through good times and bad. We need others in our lives to feel validated. Sometimes we need them to help us feel safe or simply to share our life experiences.

When your relationships become awkward, stunted, distant, or broken in some way, it can cause a great deal of hurt and despair. Feelings of loss, loneliness, unworthiness, confusion, frustration, depression, or even anger are common in this situation. You might be at a total loss for how to heal a relationship that started out so well.

Perhaps a misunderstanding has ballooned so far out of control that a close friend cuts off all communication, refusing to give you the chance to explain properly. Or maybe every family get-together seems like a chore that weighs you down when you'd rather be spending your precious time with people who understand you.

It's so upsetting when you have no idea how to mend fences or how to communicate with people in your life who seem so different. At worst, when a relationship fails, your life may seem to lack meaning until you can move beyond the hurt.

If your relationships are causing frustration, sadness, or any of these feelings, this book will help you view yourself and your relationships from angles you may never have considered.

Take heart, because it is fully possible to learn new ways of having successful, supportive relationships with the people in your life who mean the most to you. It is possible to turn even severely broken relationships in a positive direction.

You can revitalize your relationships and reap the benefits of having satisfied, supportive, encouraging, and even soulful connections with others in your life.

Why do relationships go so wrong?

We all have common behavior patterns and patterns of communicating that we consider perfectly normal. These patterns are taught to us by society—but in truth, they lead to great distress in our relationships.

Although prevalent, they are counterproductive. Because they are so common, we don't even notice them—they are completely hidden from our conscious thought.

For example, we may have grown up in a family where it was OK to judge and criticize others. Perhaps the whole family chimes in with agreement, so it seems right. Everyone is doing it, so we don't question our pattern. This is just one pattern that will in time sabotage our relationships.

Some of the patterns cause knee-jerk reactions that ripple out and cause longer-term damage. Or they might result in counter-reactions from others that boomerang back immediately, escalating anger and arguments.

One pattern always leaves one relationship partner at a disadvantage, becoming a habit that can be uncomfortable for both partners but difficult to see and to break.

Another pattern brings other parties into the relationship to diffuse tension. This might improve the primary relationship temporarily, but the issues still exist, and ultimately must either be addressed or permitted to continue, causing discomfort for everyone.

We all use these patterns not only because we are familiar with them, but because they work—at first. But as we continue to use them, trust and communication break down and the patterns backfire, resulting in strained and often broken relationships.

It's hard to anticipate what actions on our part might cause discomfort, fear, anger, or resentment on the part of a friend or someone we love. That's because it's difficult to put ourselves into someone else's shoes. We tend to think and act from our own viewpoints, and only learn we've offended someone after the fact—after it's too late. The same thing happens in reverse, with others being unable to anticipate our feelings when they speak or act.

The good news is, there is hope for our relationships. Once we learn improved ways to act and communicate, we can develop more successful relationships that avoid the bumps and bruises caused by old ways of communicating.

This book will help you to uncover the hidden patterns you and others are using that may be sabotaging your potentially successful relationships.

If you find that you practice most or all the patterns you will learn about, take heart—this means you have flexibility. It will be easier for you to grow and change. Those who practice only one pattern may find it harder to make changes. They will simply need more assistance. If they have motivation and determination to succeed, they will have what they need to reach their goal.

How can you make your relationships go right?

For each relationship pattern or habit that fails to work well, this book will teach you multiple ways to reverse the pattern or habit. These ways will not seem too foreign or awkward. They arise from consideration and love and are comfortable to use.

The book will empower you to improve just one relationship or many. Since the new patterns you will develop are universally applicable, they will improve your experience with any type of relationship. This includes your relationship with yourself (do you ever beat yourself up in your mind?), and with others at home, your friends, people at work, in your neighborhood, or on a larger stage such as your community.

To begin anew in your relationships, you will learn through examples, through explanation, and through your own thoughtful consideration how to take the first steps to understand where the problems in your relationships lie and how to untangle them.

You will learn that although we all contribute to relationship problems, it's not anyone's fault. There is no need to assign blame. The answers are much more positive.

Good communication plays a major role in making our relationships work, but there is much more to successful relationships than this. You will learn to find gentle ways to turn things around. Sometimes even stepping back and letting go can free up enough space in a relationship to work wonders.

You will develop new attitudes and awareness through the examples and explanations in this book and through self-reflection. You'll be able to:

- **Envision the big picture,** understanding the whole situation—the forces affecting your friend or loved one that go way beyond your own personal relationship.
- **Dedicate yourself to your important people,** even when they make mistakes out of high emotion or stress. You'll patiently, persistently reach out to connect, which is potent for healing breaks in your relationships. It is not easy. But you will encounter successful methods in the chapters to come.
- **Know how to weed through relationship chaos in times of stress.** Understanding triangles will help you strengthen your one-to-one relationships.
- **Avoid the long-term downside of the overdoing and underdoing pattern** that at first feels like love, but

once ingrained as a habit causes increasing resentment and difficulty.

We all have more than one relationship. We have networks. You'll learn how to cull and grow your networks continually to surround yourself with people who are willing and able to be mutually supportive.

What's more, the solutions in this book will make your networks, whether they include family, friends, neighbors, or coworkers, so much more effective. Because the new patterns and solutions work so well, it takes only one person to change what they're doing to effect positive change in the other members of any group. As one person gains in maturity, others gradually take on more mature behavior as well.

If you are the person taking steps to encourage change, you'll feel pleased and gratified to gradually see the others in your group interacting happily and spreading good will with each other rather than the criticism or barbs that once may have dominated their interactions.

The importance of change

Improving your life requires change and motivation. As you begin to change by applying the principles in this book, it will become a self-reinforcing process. Even if sometimes change feels awkward, your progress will encourage you to continue these positive changes.

This book will give you ample motivation. Until then, just relax about changing and go forward with a curious mindset.

What are the secrets to relationship success?

The real first secret to successful relationships begins with our relationship with ourselves. We all have certain chronic anxieties (we are often unaware of) that make it difficult for us to navigate relationships under stress. And relationships are often under stress.

When one person with underlying anxieties interacts with another person with anxieties, you can guess what happens—the two react emotionally. It's a recipe for disaster when it comes to getting along over the long term in a stressful environment.

So the first secret is that it's essential to identify and deal with our own anxieties in order to develop emotional maturity. By desensitizing ourselves to anxieties we're holding onto, and by reprocessing or reframing the information stored in our subconscious, we can participate in relationships differently—more effectively.

Rather than reacting emotionally when a friend or loved one approaches us in an uncomfortable way, we can step back and determine the best way to handle the situation.

This approach calls for other success secrets which include realizing when it is best not to take action or comment personally. First, invite them to explain their views about the subject.

This can take time and requires the cooperation of both parties. But you can gain your friend's cooperation using a calm, inclusive, nonjudgmental approach. You also will learn other secrets to success throughout the book that you can begin to use. You will begin to see results from the start.

A structure to improve human behavior

According to Murray Bowen, a psychiatrist and scientist, emotional maturity results from a person's ability to differentiate themselves or to think like an individual while still being meaningfully connected with others. It's an ability to balance one's emotions and intelligence, being true to oneself while giving others room to be true to their unique selves.

To learn how emotional maturity is achieved, Bowen observed and thought about emotionally-mature people he knew. He was aware of their successful relationships. He thought about the processes they used when faced with conflict.

This process, along with Bowen's earlier studies, resulted in Bowen family systems theory. My thirty-five years of practice helping others to greatly improve their relationships and their lives is grounded in this theory.

Bowen theory will help you discover practical aspects of emotional maturity that will empower you to feel lighter, more hopeful, more capable. Bowen found that people making this effort eventually become the one others turn to for advice. Thus, your growing inner strengths will be noticed and reflected back to you by others.

Fifteen years into my practice I discovered a second key healing approach I've used to help my clients make quantum leaps in the process of improving their relationships. I've been using EMDR (eye movement desensitization and reprocessing) therapy with clients successfully for twenty years.

You may have heard of EMDR therapy. It is often used for PTSD, but it's not limited to helping PTSD alone. EMDR enables people to rapidly resolve events or issues that have impacted their mind, emotions, and even physical sensations, whether the events happened just weeks or years in the past.

Through a process of reprocessing conscious and subconscious information from key experiences, this therapy promotes the empowerment of your best brain in ways you will understand after reading this book. EMDR provides better access to your strengths and talents that you may have forgotten but not lost.

When I received EMDR training in 1997, I could see the great potential to help Bowen theory become more efficient. I could see my clients make efficient breakthroughs they rarely did through Bowen alone.

So, although Murray Bowen did not believe in protocols, I created a protocol to combine or integrate the two methods. I call it iBE (integrative Bowen and EMDR). I've found that integrating the two approaches helps people progress in their relationships with a speed and naturalness that has been remarkable to both clients and myself. See appendix 1 for more information about how iBE therapy was developed.

A protocol can have great value. The EMDR approach, when integrated with Bowen in iBE, has the capacity to increase differentiation of self or emotional maturity more quickly. "It's like Bowen on steroids!" as one therapist reported after she applied iBE with clients for a few months.

I have since practiced and researched an iBE group protocol to serve an urgent need for greater numbers of people to progress more efficiently, and at a lower cost.

What drew me to Bowen theory? A personal story

It can be helpful and interesting to understand how the process you might use to change your life was developed.

When I was in my social work graduate program at the University of Minnesota, as the eldest child, my mother told me my dad had lost his architectural business owing to a large Midwest recession. He was fifty-seven-years-old, and so depressed he was sitting around doing nothing. He had always expected to die at fifty-seven, the same age his father had suddenly died of a heart attack.

This eventually impacted me, because I was so worried about my beloved father that I became depressed. It is a long story that I will tell in the next book about going deeper into emotional maturity.

However, I can tell you now that it took only three sessions of family therapy for my father's depression to lift as he found a job and renewed his lease on life. He lived for thirty-two more years.

I found family therapy, and my Bowen experience so effective that I chose to use it exclusively in my own practice with clients after graduation. I've also turned to a Bowen coach any time I've had a major challenge in my own life I couldn't handle readily on my own. My personal efforts and those guided by my coaches have been very rewarding, helping me to improve many relationships or situations. And my clients have also benefitted greatly.

You need EMDR for that

Fifteen years later I chose the efficient and effective EMDR approach, again, through my personal experience.

Despite having Bowen's excellent theory to guide me, after I started a private practice my clientele eventually fell off. I felt like a failure. Rather than face my fear of marketing which petrified me, I found a job. In 1997, the desire to be in private practice returned, although with trepidation.

"I'm afraid of another failure," I confided to a dear friend.

She said, "Oh, you need EMDR for that!"

I asked her, "What's that?"

She said, "EMDR is amazing!" and referred me to her EMDR therapist, Belle.

Belle gave me the first phase of the EMDR protocol—the responsible and thorough history session—and prepared me for EMDR work (the second phase). Based on my history and my results with the self-help techniques, she gave me the rest of the eight-phase EMDR protocol during our second, ninety-minute session.

I was delighted to find that all my fears of private practice disappeared during that session. My therapy was done. With this, I proved the initial research published by Francine Shapiro, EMDR's developer. Shapiro found that those who experience single-event trauma can resolve it in one-to-three ninety-minute EMDR sessions.

I immediately registered for the training to become an EMDR therapist.

Shapiro encouraged therapists to integrate our EMDR practice with the other specialties we worked with. My goal has been to let the efficiency of EMDR improve the value of Bowen theory for my clients. It helps them improve their emotional maturity, and as a result, their relationships transform on all levels.

Emotional maturity is the ability to be true to yourself despite the pressures from others to fit in. It also implies the ability to let others be different, while being able to set boundaries on behavior when necessary.

Soon after completing EMDR training, I combined Bowen and EMDR to develop what I eventually called Integrative Bowen and EMDR, or iBE. The goal of iBE is to address Bowen's categories of anxiety-binding mechanisms, or relationship ouches, with EMDR therapy. You will learn all about Bowen's anxiety-binding mechanisms (ABMs) in this book. It is these often-hidden mechanisms that tear apart our relationships.

Whether used with individuals or groups, iBE helps to neutralize distress about past events, and then educate people about healthier ways to handle similar issues using Bowen theory.

This endeavor of using iBE with clients occupied me for ten years, after which I began to share my methods with other EMDR therapists. After developing a group iBE protocol in 2016 and researching the results, I am now ready to share my work with you.

Who will be helped by this book

This book is written in a user-friendly language, taking care to avoid psycho-babble and other language that might put off or confuse people.

The book will serve the lay person who wants greater success and peace in their relationships. Bowen's principles can become a roadmap through life, helping you figure out the useful detours to take when roadblocks are put up, or construction gets too chaotic. I hope you will find your life becoming more empowered and contented, and your relationships becoming more vital, useful resources for support, fun, and greater understanding.

The book will also serve therapists curious to learn what can happen when integrating these two powerful healing approaches for the benefit of their own clients.

Bowen himself and therapists dedicated to Bowen's theory often share their own stories of working on self in their families. I've learned valuable lessons through this practice. Thus, therapists will find that I share more about self than the average therapist. My goal is not to meet my own needs for attention, but to give examples that may give hope and encouragement to others. It can be comforting to learn about the struggles and eventual progress made by others.

I invite Bowen therapists to read my take on Bowen theory. Since much of my training is through the oral tradition of working with therapist-coaches trained by Bowen or his trainees, I have found my experiences and stories can differ from that of other Bowen enthusiasts. In fact, very dedicated Bowen leaders have heard stories from Bowen that contradicted other stories he shared. I cannot resolve these discrepancies, but I can share that the principles and stories I've learned have helped me in my life and helped my clients as well. Please refer to appendix 1 for more information about how iBE therapy draws from both Bowen theory and EMDR therapy.

Navigating this book

Chapter structure

The first two chapters of this book will help you see the big picture—the widespread nature of relationship problems and the potential for resolution now, for our future, and for the lives of our future generations.

Chapter 2 delves into the details of Bowen theory and EMDR therapy to help you understand the reasons behind the changes recommended to improve your life. It's important to understand the why before learning how to implement any theory.

Chapters 3 through 10 are organized to help you discover and understand the hidden relationship-sabotaging anxiety-binding mechanisms (ABMs) identified by Bowen, and choose maturity-building principles (MBPs, named by me) to replace them and reverse the ABMs. Maturity-building principles value difference, and understanding the differences.

The odd-numbered chapters in this range explain the ABMs, the routes to avoid, and the even numbered chapters, plus chapter 11 provide you with the relationship-saving antidotes. This is your roadmap to recovery.

Chapter 11 describes a helpful step-by-step skill: how to use "I" positions with others to clarify your needs and position in any relationship. "I" positions are not a one-way street. They are a starting point to help you gain clarity and confidence, introduce that information into the relationship, and then proceed to communicate with the other(s) to negotiate an appropriate route that honors all parties involved. "I" positions help us to create healthy boundaries with others.

Relevant quotations

Each chapter is introduced by short list of quotations to affirm the value of the principle or concept embraced by that chapter and to make you think.

I selected these verses and thoughts from a variety of world scriptures and noble leaders to help you see that neither Murray Bowen nor any other single source invented the principles of emotional maturity.

Bowen and other leaders simply did a great job of observing the principles of emotional maturity and helping us consciously grow them in our lives.

Emotional maturity means the ability to stay true to oneself, to one's cherished principles above all. Yet it also means to attend to one's feelings and opinions, to take them into account and let them digest before taking action. This requires calm patience, allowing principles to be remembered and practiced with consistency.

Emotional maturity includes being true to others, committed to relationships whether they be family, friend, coworker, or neighbor. Emotionally-mature people thus have a strong set of connections, yielding a vital support system.

Those of lesser maturity follow intense emotion rather than guiding values and beliefs. This causes temporary amnesia of one's principles, the loss of consistency and reliability, and losing the trust of others.

Bowen's theory offers a simple, comprehensive understanding and perspective. Although the principles are simple to understand, they are not always simple to practice. Many truths and factors are involved in all situations in all families. Viewing our situations from many angles helps us to comprehend the bigger picture and embrace a true understanding.

Regarding the scriptures, by including quotations from different religions I am not promoting any religion in particular. We live in a world with diverse religions, each with its own inspiring culture that is natural and beautiful for its followers. I have great respect for these differences.

Yet, there is also a great unity among the religions. I have tried to demonstrate this through the selected verses. The same concepts are described in delightfully varied vocabularies. You can also find a very tangible example of this in appendix 3, The Golden Rule.

George Washington's wisdom

Through his noble character, George Washington earned the love and admiration of friends and foes, Americans, native chiefs, and foreign diplomats. That is why he is given a seat of honor at a table illumined by the light of wisdom.

The behaviors Washington practiced are described in the beginning quotes I've credited to George Washington. They were published as George Washington's *Rules of Civility & Decent Behavior in Company and Conversation.*

In truth, they are thought to be the result of a penmanship exercise completed when he was sixteen. He was copying rules embraced by the French Jesuits since 1595.

Some of the rules so promote the consideration of others' sensibilities that many twenty-first century readers may find it extreme or even silly. However, the principles of consideration

and respect of others promotes a deep understanding of the
equality of all. These principles should never become outdated.

One of Washington's most enthusiastic admirers, Parson
Weems, wrote of him:

> No wonder everybody honoured him who honoured
> every body. . . . No wonder everybody loved him who,
> by his unwearied attention to the public good,
> manifested the tenderest love for everybody.

Oprah Winfrey and Mother Teresa

Oprah Winfrey is the single most commonly-respected female
figure my clients spontaneously mention as a healing figure.

Sometimes in EMDR therapy we use imagination to replay a
memory to get your needs met this time. I ask, "Imagine your
mother or father was able to be and do for you what you
needed."

Some people can to this. But for those whose mothers were so
blocked and traumatized, or cruel and violent that they can't
imagine getting their needs met through that mother, I ask
them to choose an alternate. Oprah is the number one choice.
Mother Teresa is a close second. That is why both are
represented here.

Pop quizzes

Following the quotes, each chapter presents a pop quiz to get
your mind in gear for some of the possibilities to be gained in
that chapter. Some statements don't have an absolute right
answer because you are being asked to reflect about your own
experience.

Appendix 2 includes a key of answers representing Bowen
theory-inspired ideals to reach for, but please don't think of
your answers as either right or wrong based on those ideals.

If you find confirmation in the direction you are going, or you become interested in working toward the ideal, then taking the quiz was a useful, introspective exercise.

Reversing societal regression

In the 1970s, Bowen observed a societal regression, which is the opposite of increasing emotional maturity. He predicted this general trend would continue, causing cycles of crises coming with faster speed until the middle of the twenty-first century.

As we are experiencing increasing climate disasters, a declining state of public discourse, and other indicators, it does appear the regression is snowballing.

The goal of this book is to plant seeds for overcoming the regression. May these seeds be like oak acorns, growing a stately inner guidance system in each one who takes on the challenge.

It is important for emotionally-mature, differentiated people to be clear regarding their values, beliefs, opinions, feelings, and decisions. I believe living in this way offers hope of reversing the regression.

Limits and Options

Integrative Bowen and EMDR is an understanding, a knowledgeable approach to your relationship with yourself and your relationships with others. You will find here a self-directed discipline for principled living that balances responsibility for self with responsibility for others.

This is a self-help book that I hope you will use as a practical roadmap for a more successful and peaceful journey through your life. Each chapter ends with two sections. An *At a Glance* summary of key points will make it easier for you to review and hold on to the principles. *Practical Tips* provides suggested activities you can do to apply the chapter concepts to your own situation.

When I Do Relationships So Right, How Do They Go So Wrong? will educate you about two powerful approaches to greater health for your whole being, with its physical, mental, emotional, and spiritual aspects. If you find the self-directed method sometimes is too difficult a discipline, it may be a sign that you have self-limiting beliefs that originated in distressing past experiences. If you find your relationship challenges are complex and distressing, or provoke more anxiety than you want to face on your own, please find an iBE therapist or a Bowen therapist to help smooth your way through the emotional jungle.

Stories of my life and the lives of my clients and their families are shared here with identifying details including names and locations. These have been changed when necessary or requested to protect confidentiality.

Imagine

We all do our best in relationships because we care. We have learned from people who also did their best. However, our relationship education consists mostly of witnessing untrained people following unconscious habits. It doesn't always go well. Sometimes relationships work. Sometimes they don't. Of course we can easily blame others when relationships fail. But there's that nagging question that comes in the quiet of the night: "Am I playing a part here?"

That question becomes a key for growth. If we become more conscious of the patterns we practice in a dance with the patterns of others, we gain the power to change our part. In that lies much hope.

As we walk this path, we touch others. Our thoughtful touches ripple to people connected to them and beyond. As we become truer to ourselves and those we are connected to, in time others find our changes appealing enough to follow suit.

Let's dream a little. Imagine this happening on a big scale and rippling through the generations.

Chapter 1
Thinking Big—The Seventh Generation Principle

"The Lord . . . visits the iniquity of the fathers on the children and the children's children, to the third and the fourth generation."

Exodus 34:67, Deuteronomy 5:8-10

"What if we visit the integrity of the fathers and mothers on the children and the children's children to the third, fourth, and even seventh generations?"

Dana Elken Terrell

"Washington's mind is great and powerful, his penetration strong, no judgment was ever sounder. His integrity is most pure, his justice the most inflexible I have ever known. He is, indeed, in every sense of the words, a wise, a good and a great man."

Thomas Jefferson

"To live by this [the Seventh Generation] principle, one would ask, prior to any undertaking, how it will affect the land, water, air, animals, birds, plants, and the future for our children seven generations into the future?"

Molly Larkin, 2013

We, the International Council of Thirteen Indigenous Grandmothers, represent a global alliance of prayer, education, and healing for our Mother Earth, all her inhabitants, all the children, and for the next seven generations to come.

grandmotherscouncil.org, 2018

A story of three generations

Act I

In the small town of Portland, North Dakota, Lucille's sweet
sister was born when Lucille was nine years old. Having been
the youngest of three, with two older brothers, Lucille was very
excited to have little Jeannie to love and care for.

Lucille became a second mother to her sister, particularly
because their mother had arthritis, and found it hard in her late
forties to hold the growing baby with Down syndrome. By the
time Jeannie was six, she was still very dependent on her
mothers.

No one knew how to optimize the development of such a child
in 1943. Lucille thrilled to teach Jeannie how to write her
name, but had to reteach her again and again. Jeannie kept
forgetting.

One day after school, Lucille ran through the home looking for
her sister. "Jeannie, Jeannie!" When Jeannie was nowhere to
be seen, her parents explained, "She's been brought to the
Grafton State School, at the advice of Uncle Roy and a social
worker. They have a rule that we can't visit for a month to give
Jeannie time to adjust to her new home."

Lucille was heartbroken. And angry! She was mad at her
mother, Ruth, her father, Carl, her uncle, and the social
worker—all the grownups. She felt helpless.

The month crawled by until *Visit Jeannie Day* arrived. Lucille
tried to act as adult as a fifteen-year-old can, but she was
actually quivering, so eager to take her little Jeannie in her
arms.

Following a nurse at the school, Lucille led the family through
the long hospital halls until she reached the ward which was
now Jeannie's home. The nurse in white walked with echoing

clip, clip, clip, clips further down the hall to the playroom where Jeannie sat on the floor.

"Jeannie! We're here!" Jeannie looked up with a blank look on her face. She searched the family surrounding her and reached her arms up to Mother. "Mommy," she whispered. Lucille was in shock.

Later, Lucille cried in the back seat all the way home. Her parents didn't say a word. This wasn't unusual for her father, but not for her mom. Poor Lucille was totally confused by everything going on. But the coolness of her loving mother was inconceivable.

Before the trip ended, Lucille was furious at all the grownups involved in this. She could see where the situation was headed. Feeling totally hopeless about Jeannie—and completely devastated—she felt forced to conclude she no longer had a sister.

It wasn't long before all signs of Jeannie were removed from the home—her clothes, her photos from the walls and albums, and her name from conversation.

Act II

During high school, Lucille became the beauty of Portland. At a local roller skating rink, she met the handsome prince of nearby Mayville. They fell in love and married. They eagerly welcomed the birth of the first of their four children, Louise. This was the first baby in Lucille's life since Jeannie.

Louise has a very early memory. There was something stiff about the way her mother held her. From Lucille's perspective, she remembers that her toddler Louise shook off her touch and ran away.

One day when Louise was fifteen, she started to cry herself to sleep, mourning something that seemed lost. She didn't know what. Finally, mother Lucille heard her and came in, "Oh, what's wrong? What's wrong!"

"Mom, you never hug me."

"I can't, I just can't." Lucille left and closed the door behind her.

Act III

"I never want to be like you!" Louise's teen rampage assaulted Lucille's ears.

Ten years of smoldering, testy conversations expressed Louise's disappointment and Lucille's helplessness. Finally, a crack of light opened in the armor. Lucille told Louise about Jeannie.

Louise was stunned. She had always thought there were three children in her mother's family. She thought Lucille was the only girl. Instantly she understood that her mother was afraid that if she loved too much, those she loved would be taken from her. She only held back her love—because she loved.

Act IV

Lucille died in 2003. In 2005, Lucille's sister-in-law, her brother Bob's widow, shared with Louise and her sisters what they had never known about Jeannie.

As a high school senior, Bobbie had returned home early the day Jeannie went to the state school to find his mother alone in the garden crying, "Jeannie, Jeannie, Jeannie." He rushed to her to ask what was wrong.

He learned that his father and Uncle Roy decided Jeannie needed to go, and Mother had no choice in the matter. She didn't want the children to know their father would do such a thing, so she swore Bob to secrecy. He told only his wife, who revealed the secret to Lucille's daughters after his passing.

Struggling with a lifelong mystery

Louise felt impelled to become a therapist to understand the mysteries of her mother and herself, of love, and life. She is now impelled to write this book to help others understand the mystery people in their lives and loves. The mystery of Louise is that her full name is Dana Louise Elken Terrell.

Virtue and maturity come from considering the well-being of the greatest number. Carl, my grandfather, never reached that level of emotional maturity, that ability to consider so many people. He believed he was sending Jeannie away for the good of his wife. But since he didn't discuss it with her, it created a trust wound that never healed. It seems Carl did not consider the effects on the rest of his family. He also felt embarrassed about this less-than-perfect daughter. So, he may have been meeting his own need to make life easier for himself.

Poor Carl became a broken, grumpy man. I didn't like being around him at all. He died when I was twelve, so I never got the chance to know him more deeply.

Carl's sad decision left a lingering effect on himself, his wife, his children's generation, and me and my generation. We were raised by a mother whose traumatic loss of Jeannie was closely followed by the unresponsiveness of her previously loving parents. The combination deeply wounded her heart and its full capacity for love.

A psychological theory to help future generations

I didn't know about Carl's choice, but nevertheless experienced the consequences of it in my relationship with my mother. What can we learn from the long-term fallout of others' stress and trauma?

I didn't learn much until I was introduced to Bowen family systems theory in graduate school.

Psychiatrist Murray Bowen, even as a child, was a natural problem solver. When he entered the field of medicine, he considered the available specialties to see where the greatest problems were. He selected psychiatry. Most other fields were based on solid science. In the late forties and fifties, he did not believe that claim could be confidently asserted for psychiatry.

Initially he was trained in Freudian psychoanalysis. Bowen was not satisfied with its effectiveness. He believed part of the problem was psychoanalysis relied on Freud guessing what was going on in the patient's unconscious mind. This was not based on science. Bowen could see for himself that early and current family relationships affected people greatly, and Freudians were largely ignoring these two developmental stages.

In the 1950s, Bowen researched whole families having a schizophrenic member. He took advantage of the fact that research money was available to study this unique problem. Bowen sought families willing to enter the hospital together with the schizophrenic family member. He hoped this research would shed light on the problem of schizophrenia, bringing better outcomes. But he also hoped the lessons learned would have universal benefits rather than being specific to a unique population.

Bowen's first research question was, "How do human beings respond to stress?" The researchers observed four basic patterns of behavior, which Bowen called anxiety-binding mechanisms (ABMs). They might be called the ouches in relationships:

1. Conflict (see chapter 3)
2. Distance (see chapter 5)
3. Triangling—or Bringing in a Third (see chapter 7)
4. Overfunctioning/Underfunctioning Reciprocity, or One Up/One Down (see chapter 9)

Bowen's researchers admitted to him they could relate to these ABMs, and that they used them in their own lives from time to time. Bowen was happy to hear this, because he knew his researchers were fairly well-functioning individuals. If the theory could apply to a schizophrenic at a low level of functioning and also to others functioning well, perhaps it qualified as a universal theory of psychology.

Seeing the similarity between the two groups, Bowen also observed the differences. The higher functioning people used the anxiety-binding mechanisms less frequently and less intensely than the lower functioning people.

He hypothesized that these differences in intensity were inversely related to the degree of emotional maturity, or differentiation of self. Emotional maturity and differentiation of self are defined as the ability to be a unique individual while in connection with significant others. So, as differentiation of self or emotional maturity increase, people use ABMs less intensely and vice versa.

An individual's level of maturity is a result of the level of maturity of his parents, combined with the amount of anxious focus directed at him as he matures, plus the weight of stressors or traumas the family experienced during his lifetime and in the eighteen months or so before he was born. However, the traumas of the past generations also can have a noticeable effect.

As for Carl

Unfortunately, we know little about Carl's parents. We only know of his father's horrific sudden death at the dinner table, witnessed by the whole family. His father suffered from throat cancer.

After his father's death, Carl's mother gave fifteen-year-old Carl the responsibility to be head of the household. These two successive traumas likely froze his emotional development at the level of a fifteen-year-old. He was forced to pretend maturity without the ideal opportunity to reach that state slowly and naturally.

Having this perspective makes Carl look less distasteful, less bad or marked by iniquity. Exodus 34:37 refers to the "iniquity of the fathers." If we replace the word iniquity with the phrase, habits or patterns, our own thinking can become less judgmental and more neutral—we can have more understanding for habits or patterns of the fathers. This is a worthwhile exercise, as we contemplate the people in our own families who have a bad rap.

Much fear was associated with schizophrenia in the 1950s. At that time, a new theory ascribed the blame to the mother, who was labeled a schizophrenogenic mother.

Dr. Bowen was surprised to learn through his studies that neither the patient nor the family members exhibited the fixed characteristics described by previous psychology research.

Instead, he found that people's behavior patterns and functioning could change dramatically. With a little wise feedback based on Bowen theory from a trusted coach (Bowen's preferred term for therapists), the changes could eventually go in a direction that was stable and beneficial for each member of the family.

Applying Bowen theory

Speaking from my own experience, coping with the anxiety-binding mechanisms is quite a challenge. Thus, in this book I devote one chapter to each relationship ouch, followed by a chapter on what I call the maturity-building principles, described by Bowen's observation and thinking about the emotionally-mature people he knew. Though this effort was informal and could not be called research, it may be one of the earliest studies of emotional health.

The more people can gain perspective about these ouch patterns, understand their part in them, and learn new options available to them, the more they can be in the driver's seat in their own lives.

When we take responsibility for our side of the equation, guided by Bowen theory, others who are connected to us cannot help but change a bit themselves. They may naturally start to take responsibility for their side of the equation.

This happens because we operate within a system, something like a web. All it takes is one motivated person, consciously and consistently working on self within relationships, to gradually help those relationships.

Bowen theory requires neither pushing nor forcing another to change. It only asks the motivated person to nudge themselves to change.

A theory ahead of its time

Bowen's curious mind and research led him to think bigger than most other psychiatrists of his day, although a few other pioneers in family systems theory were also exploring this systems way of viewing families.

While Freudian psychiatrists were peering into individuals to discover their unconscious tendencies, Bowen looked broadly at the entire extended family system. He looked back into the patterns in past generations as far back as his patients had history, whether that was three generations or ten.

The principles of Bowen family systems theory came from his research, his personal experience, and his observation and deep thinking about emotionally-mature people familiar to him. He was one of the first to describe what emotional health looks like. This is valuable because it is hard to reach a goal if you don't have a clear idea of the destination.

Dr. Roberta Gilbert is a Bowen student who has written excellent introductions to the theory for laypeople. Bowen's theory has helped therapists and their clients to gain relationships she calls "extraordinary" (Gilbert, 1992).

I have practiced this theory for more than thirty-five years. So far, it has never let me down.

Bowen and his chief proponents have been less interested in collecting data from research than in researching the principles in their own lives. Thus, the proponents speak with conviction and earn trust easily.

The downside of this is that in the Bowen discussions here, you will find precious few of the statistical validations you are used to finding from a self-help book about the psychology of relationships. Nonetheless, you will find that Bowen proponents have a solid reason for their convictions. They, like I, have put the theory to the test in the laboratory of their own lives.

Like the ancient rishis and sages of India and Persia, Bowen enthusiasts have received guidance from a master (or a Bowen coach) and continued to bring our practice of principles as close to an authentic core as possible.

Bowen theory uses the same training method, basically a mentorship relationship, that protected these two ancient cultures against the cultural demise that eventually befell Egypt, Babylonia, Greece, and Rome. It has produced men and women of virtue in each generation.

Gandhi is a most famous example. He led and won a war against the British Empire without firing a shot.

Bowen theory and schizophrenia

Throughout this book I will share the available research reports about Bowen, because there are a few fascinating ones.

One of the most fascinating reports concerns the development of schizophrenia. A pattern called child focus (see chapter 7, Triangling—or Bringing in a Third) was prevalent in the researched families. This term doesn't mean simply focusing on children's necessities. That is, of course, essential for parents to do for their children. Bowen's term means an over-focus. It is a matter of degree.

Bowen learned that families with a child focus pattern created at least one weakened individual in each generation. Whether the focus was positive, negative, or worried, it somewhat did the child in.

In child focus, the weakness, anxiety, or insecurities of the parents are projected onto one or more in the next generation. Bowen called this the family projection process.

Bowen observed that individuals tended to mate with a person of equal maturity level. They then focused their somewhat anxious attention on at least one offspring. The offspring then repeated the pattern. Thus far no additional research (Miller, 2004) has proven or disproven this assertion.

When the context of high stress was added to the child focus, Bowen's research team found it could take three generations of child focus to result in the behaviors and thought patterns of schizophrenia. If the context included a period of very low environmental stress, the same pattern could take ten generations to produce schizophrenia.

Again, I've not been able to find collaborative or disputing evidence regarding this assertion since Bowen's research from the 1950s. This is unfortunate, because such a significant discovery deserves to be researched further. Bowen himself played some role in the lack of research. He discouraged the development (Miller, 2004) of a measure of emotional maturity, as he thought it was impossible to measure without months of interviews by trained clinicians.

To my knowledge, by 2017 no one has developed an interview tool which could standardize the interview process that Bowen believed in. However, Skowron (1998) developed the Differentiation of Self Inventory to measure emotional maturity. Thus, it is a worthy subject for research.

Bowen called the phenomenon he observed in the family histories of those in his study, the multigenerational transmission process. This process doesn't require a pattern of child focus (it can apply to any of Bowen's anxiety-binding mechanisms) but the child focus pattern is a key to understanding schizophrenia. Miller (2004) also made the point that schizophrenia is not the only disorder or symptom that can arise from child focus.

The good news? This discovery guided Bowen to help parents change the pattern they were practicing, to lift the focus off their child and onto the parental relationship. This allowed the diagnosed offspring to naturally continue the work of growing an independent self. He also coached the family to work together to solve their problems.

Bowen avoided the expert point of view in which the expert takes too much responsibility, leaving the clients in a one down position (see chapter 9, Understanding One Up/One Down Reciprocity). This was a significant way Bowen patiently made room for the existing strengths of the family to expand.

Dr. Bowen shared an example of this process (Bowen, 1957, 1957a, Bowen, 1978, 41). One case began nine months into therapy, as the mother began realizing how much of her mental time she used to concentrate on her daughter (who had been diagnosed with schizophrenia during her freshman year in college in the 1950s). The mother started to get curious about this and wondered why she tended to have the same feelings as her daughter. They were so close it was as if they did not have separation.

Bowen used the term fused to describe this phenomenon. The daughter was aware of the fusion of feelings, too. She relied on her mother to let her know how she felt, how she looked, etc.

The mother decided to "put an invisible wall between us so I can have my life and she can have hers."

When the daughter went to college, she began to have some feelings of her own. But she could easily get confused if an authority figure suggested how she should feel.

Though Bowen guided the mother and daughter to be separate and different individuals, the mother reached an aha moment when she concluded, "Parents should let their children lead their own lives." (Bowen, 1978, 41).

The daughter soon embraced this belief as well. At the next session of coaching, the daughter came in with a new hairstyle, radiating charm and self-confidence. Her parents were beaming.

Significantly, the daughter had been able to return to old friends from college days. She had feared they would place a stigma on her due to her psychotic break. Instead, though aware of her struggles, they accepted her as she was, as they did in the past. The daughter began to realize that if anyone had a problem with her, it was due to their fears of mental illness, and not a fear of her.

Once she learned to separate herself from her mother, she could also be separate from others, and not take their comments or behaviors so personally.

To this point, this example describes a weakening style of the multigenerational transmission process in families, meaning that functioning becomes weaker with subsequent generations. However, it is also possible that some offspring will remain at the same level of emotional maturity, while some will progress beyond the parents' level.

The transmission process can be positive, negative, or neutral. If it goes in a negative direction, it can always be reversed through conscious effort. This is where hope lies.

Bowen theory on a larger scale

Bowen theory helps us understand how one branch of the family might grow more successful with each generation while another branch of the family that received more parental weakness long ago, might grow more challenged with each generation.

The same process also can be observed in society as a whole. Bowen called societal weakening the societal regression process. He began "fairly serious thinking and observations about social unrest and societal regression" about 1955. "Society appeared more restless, more selfish, more immature, more lawless, and more irresponsible than in previous years." (Bowen, 1978, 270).

Bowen struggled to think calmly about this mystery. He considered and discarded a number of hypotheses. In general, he observed that societal regression couldn't be ascribed to individual issues, but to very complex factors affecting us as systems. This included the enormous population growth—a long-term process producing a decrease in emotional maturity. Our short-sightedness has produced problems that are now intense and difficult to resolve.

He wrote:

A more differentiated society would not have as serious an environmental problem as we now have. If society functioned on a higher level, we would have a higher percentage of people oriented to responsibility for self and others, and for the environment, and a lower percentage focused on rights and force and on legal mechanisms to guarantee rights. A more differentiated society could take the present environmental problems and find better solutions than will be possible in our present less differentiated state (Bowen, 1978, 449).

Begin with the end in mind

Steven Covey, in *The 7 Habits of Highly Effective People*, described what he called the success ability, which is to begin a project with a clear vision of the end goal in mind.

Perhaps we can experiment with this. What would it look like if we could consider the well-being of our environment and Mother Nature (which includes ourselves) for the next seven generations?

Bowen believed we are not differentiated or emotionally mature enough to even think of the best solutions. But I think there is great power in the imagination. Olympic athletes and their coaches have proven that imagining a perfect sports practice can be more effective for champions than actual practice.

So, let us imagine a perfect way to enhance and protect our environment. What are both small and large steps we might take to provide for greater purity of our air, water, soil, food supply? At home, we could plant an organic garden or a tree. We thus offer a gift to our neighborhood of more green leaves to pour more oxygen into the atmosphere.

Other small steps include recycling, minimizing our water use, and xeriscape landscape design. A bigger step could be choosing a fuel-efficient hybrid car or finding ways to minimize the miles we drive.

Kip Andersen became inspired to do all he could by watching the documentary, *An Inconvenient Truth.* He rode a bike and rarely drove his van. He did his best, but had a nagging feeling he wasn't doing enough. Kip embarked on a research project: an investigative documentary called *What the Health.*

My daughter-in-law is deeply committed to health as a super-busy student in a physician's assistant program. Amid a heavy schedule of finals, she watched Andersen's documentary. She became inspired to become a vegetarian, conditional on her research to see if Andersen's claims could be verified in the medical literature. She found that only one claim was not validated by her review of medical research (that eating eggs is as bad for you as smoking for decades). Thus, she has remained a vegetarian.

The film demonstrates that by reducing support of the animal agri-industry, individuals can reduce their contribution to pollution far more than any other conservation measure.

Another documentary, *Forks Over Knives,* describes the largest health study of all time called The China Study (the team included 6,000 researchers). This study demonstrates the health dangers of a meat and dairy diet. In China, diseases like cancer, heart disease, and diabetes were unknown until a Western diet with these foods was introduced.

I believe knowing and learning from the results of The China Study will help our physical health improve and thus reduce our stressors.

Take a moment to imagine what small step you could take, and perhaps a bigger step in the future, to care for and protect yourself and the coming generations.

As the pressures of the growing population increase, people have more need for connection, but also more anxiety about it. They migrate to find more space, leaving people behind. Those of us who had immigrant parents, whether in the past decade or the past century, may be aware of ways the family left others behind.

This pattern has become a national habit in the United States. Bowen observed a long-term process of cutoff (meaning having extreme distance) in significant relationships. This will receive more attention in chapter 5 on distance.

Current signs of societal regression

Have you noticed? Do relationships seem somewhat different? Is parenting different? Are our children different than they were in the past?

Daniel Papero of the Bowen Center faculty in Washington, DC says that the chief pattern adding to society's regression currently is the same pattern of child focus Bowen saw happening in families of schizophrenics.

Families are making the children the most important members of the family. In reality, the most important relationship in the family is that between the parents. If this relationship moves to a secondary position, the marriage is at risk, and stability for children lessens. The process of child focus will be addressed more fully in chapter 7.

Meanwhile, the cutoff pattern continues to do its damage in our culture. Do you find you are living in relationship bubbles or silos more of the time? At family gatherings, do you have to tiptoe around major issues to keep peace? Or is that impossible by now? Does it seem tempting just to avoid an entire wing of the family? Or is it easy to avoid them because they just don't show up?

What I have seen is a deep embracing of "I, me, and mine," and a deeper avoidance of "you, your opinions, your feelings, your values, and your reality." This causes division. It reflects the long-term cutoff.

The emotions are simmering. During the election of 2016 I didn't find the current state of affairs terribly surprising, knowing Bowen had watched the societal regression for so long. But, I found it disturbing that civil discourse had reached such a low state. At the presidential debates I heard less-reasoned arguments than before, and more attempts at domination and schoolyard style mud-slinging.

Reversing societal regression
Please bear with me during this discussion. My goal is to be objective describing the US national political tone, rather than to take a political stand. My goal is to see strengths and weaknesses on both sides.

Many voters came to the 2016 polls only to vote for what they perceived to be the lesser of two evils. The majority were not enthusiastic about either candidate. Some chose the candidate of the party that best fit their own moral principles, even though that candidate wasn't as close a match as they preferred.

I'm more concerned about the relationships between Americans, particularly between conservatives and progressives. According to a Pew Research Center survey, "An overwhelming share of those who hold highly negative views of the opposing party say that its policies are so misguided that they threaten the nation's well-being." (pewresearch.org, June 22, 2016).

Jonathan Haidt's November 2016 TED Talk is called, "Can a divided America heal?" In it, he addresses our great distrust of one another, plus the larger red flag of disgust, both of which interfere with discourse and understanding of one another. The trust will need to be regained as the first step to healing. I think Bowen would agree.

Sometimes we just need to sit together in the same room, breathe the same air, and like the mammals, "see how each other smells." (Bowen, 25th Annual Symposium, 1988).

Social psychologist Haidt again:

> I studied disgust for many years, and I think about emotions a lot. And I think that the opposite of disgust is actually love. Love is all about, [liking]. . . . Disgust is closing off, borders. Love is about dissolving walls. So personal relationships, I think, are probably the most powerful means we have. You can be disgusted by a group of people, but then you meet a particular person and you genuinely discover that they're lovely. And then gradually that chips away or changes your category as well. The tragedy is, Americans used to be much more mixed up in their towns by left-right politics. And now that it's become this great moral divide, there's a lot of evidence that we're moving to be near people who are like us politically. It's harder to find somebody who's on the other side. So they're over there, they're far away. It's harder to get to know them (Haidt, Jonathan 2016 TED Talk, "Can a divided America heal?").

Haidt and Bowen advise similar solutions for societal regression: connecting with people who are different, with rarely seen family members or strangers; listening enough to begin to understand how they view life; and sharing how you view it.

This doesn't mean you will change each other's mindset. However, it makes a big difference in overcoming the disgust and distrust—our greatest dangers—if we want to overcome societal regression.

I had a lovely experience in this practice shortly after the election when I met at Starbucks with a man of the opposite political persuasion, or so I thought. Though we chose different candidates for president, we had an enjoyable conversation—very respectful, very honest. We were surprised to see that we had a lot in common, particularly in our values systems.

Societal progression

The degree of societal regression has motivated me to publish this book at a time when I believe it is sorely needed. If Bowen is correct, the need will only increase.

Bowen theory offers hope and a practical way for societal progression, one individual at a time. It's a roadmap to overcoming regression and heading forward with greater emotional maturity. Progress is slow but steady and sure.

The effort is worthy of a dedicated, lifelong commitment, not just for you as an individual, but for those you love and care for.

EMDR therapy

This book will also introduce you to EMDR therapy. Eye movement desensitization and reprocessing is a psychotherapy approach with enough research to satisfy data lovers.

Thirty-nine randomized control studies have validated the efficacy of EMDR for child and adult PTSD, depression, and behavioral disorders. The research has satisfied the World Health Organization which recommends only two treatments for post-traumatic stress disorder. EMDR is one. CBT, or cognitive behavioral therapy is the other. It is also effective, but usually attains success in more time than EMDR treatment.

EMDR brings rapid progress as it helps the brain desensitize distressing memories and store them in a calmed state. As I see it, there is less emotional clutter in the brain after experiencing EMDR therapy. The brain scan in chapter 2 shows what that clutter looks like visually, and how the brain appears once the memories have been desensitized with EMDR.

Through EMDR we gain better access to our strengths and talents, which have been stored in the brain all along, but are hidden by the clutter.

Dr. Francine Shapiro, the developer of EMDR, calls this increased access, the activation of the brain's adaptive information processing (AIP) system.

Chapter 2 on desensitization goes deeper into EMDR Therapy.

Integrating Bowen and EMDR

I have been integrating Bowen theory and EMDR therapy in my practice since my initial EMDR training in 1997. I call this combination, integrative Bowen and EMDR therapy (iBE).

Shapiro encouraged her trainees to integrate their EMDR practice into their previous specialties. This has been a fascinating challenge. It has offered my clients increasing success over time.

I began training EMDR therapists in my iBE approach with individuals in 2009. In 2016 I created a group iBE protocol. I realized that research on iBE is necessary to make this book a more valuable self-help guide and/or preparation for iBE therapy for those who feel the need. To read the research results, you can visit ibetherapy.com/relationshipresources.

The Haudenosaunee Iroquois Confederacy's Seventh Generation principle

Bowen isn't the only one interested in a long-term societal progression and broad-scale health.

History lovers will be interested to see how long and successfully big-picture thinking has worked for the earliest people in America. The Haudenosaunee embraced the Seventh Generation principle as part of their Great Law of Peace. Their tribe has been called the Iroquois by some.

> The earliest recording of the Seventh Generation principle dates back to the Great Law of Peace of the Iroquois Confederacy created in the twelfth century. When our Founding Fathers looked for examples of effective government and human liberty upon which to model a constitution to unite the thirteen colonies, they found it in the government of the Iroquois Nation, which, at that point, had stood for hundreds of years.

> Ironically, in drafting our constitution, our founders left out one of the essential principles of the Great Law of Peace: the Seventh Generation principle.

> It is ironic, because it is the heart of this very successful model of government—the Iroquois Great Law of Peace has today stood for 1,000 years.

> It is the omission of the Seventh Generation principle and the role of women in government that led Native Americans to say that the U.S. copied the Great Law of Peace but didn't really understand it (Larkin, 2013).

In our modern day, it seems we have increased our troubles through short-term thinking. We make major decisions based more on a Presidents' Day car sale, the value of a relationship to me for the next weeks or months, or the profit picture published in the next quarterly report.

How many of us think long-term on a daily basis? How many of us consider several future generations, much less seven, as the Iroquois Nation did? What would happen if we did?

The International Council of Thirteen Indigenous Grandmothers have committed their lives and their prayers for peace and the well-being of all. The 2009 movie that tells their story is deeply moving. Its purpose is clear: *For the Next 7 Generations.*

Bowen found that by considering facts of life for the previous generations, we can move beyond blame. We see the challenges or traumas faced by our elders, and often their lack of inner or outer resources to cope with those conundrums or even traumas.

This lack of resources made life difficult for their offspring. The multigenerational transmission process carried on stress patterns through times of great difficulty. There was little opportunity to reflect and consider reviewing and re-deciding how to live.

Thus, the crises, the cruelty, depressions, addictions, etc., just got passed on. A more limited psychological view judges those elders as bad guys or mean moms.

Bowen would ask, "What makes a skunk stink?" (Bowen Center Annual Symposium, 1988). The more we understand what life was like for the skunks, the more compassion we can develop for them. Along with compassion, we gain a gentler view.

The Thirteen Grandmothers are bringing a message of compassion. When a man asked them how he might make up for the pain caused by his pioneer relatives who took land for free from the indigenous people, a Grandmother replied, "Grandson (we make relations immediately) we need to talk about the pain, and about the solutions."

Bowen-style breakthroughs in my family's three-generation story

By secretly taking little six-year-old Jeannie to Grafton State School (for the retarded) she was essentially kidnapped from her mother and the rest of the family. Since her mother didn't want the other children, including my mother Lucille, to know the truth about their father, she went along with a story that a social worker had urged them to do it this way.

Imagine Lucille's horror when I, her daughter, came along and decided to become a social worker! Mom's trauma was triggered bigtime. She had partially blamed social workers for the devastating loss of her sister.

Yet no social worker had ever been involved.

Fake news doesn't just happen on TV. It happens in families, too—even in families where honesty and high principles are generally practiced.

I never would have figured all this out without the help of Bowen's theory encouraging me to get to know members of the family more fully, to learn facts, dates, and answers to questions about who, what, when, and where. Once I understood, I could no longer blame my mother for her ways. Instead, I understood her. This created softness between us.

As I learned Carl's story, I couldn't blame him, either. I had to look at his parents to understand him better.

Shortly after his family moved from North Dakota to Washington state, Carl's father, Evan, contracted throat cancer and quickly died a horrific death. The whole family witnessed it. Carl's grieving mother was not prepared at the turn of the nineteenth century to support a family. She gave grieving Carl the job of becoming the family breadwinner at fifteen.

Does that number sound familiar? Carl's daughter, Lucille, lost her sister at age fifteen, due to his decision. His granddaughter, Dana, felt a painfully perceivable loss of her own mother's affection at age fifteen.

As an EMDR therapist, I've witnessed similar patterns over the generations in my own clients. I believe that when our children reach the age we were when an unresolved trauma occurred, we are at risk to behave in ways that stress them.

Thus, I believe we have a responsibility to tackle our own unresolved stresses, losses, and traumas. It will help us bring our best strengths and talents into all our endeavors. EMDR therapy has been an efficient and effective way for many to do that, including myself.

On a personal level, Bowen's theory helped me see people with an expanded view. It helped me to take my focus off my own sensitivity and lack of neutrality, off how "I was hurt!" or "how Mom and Grandma Ruth were hurt!" and onto a much broader, more neutral view of all the real people involved and the complex difficulties they faced as well.

One tool to help gain a broader view for yourself is to draw a family diagram, or family tree, in which you look for and note the patterns used in the generations of your family. You can watch a video about how to do this at ibetherapy.com/relationshipresources.

The simple change of gaining a broad view, including the lives of my relatives, has given me a better level of emotional maturity, and consequently far more satisfying and successful relationships than I could have formed in my natural mode.

Creating societal progression

At the societal level, Bowen helps us see it's not helpful to assign blame for societal regression. The cause is better placed on the practice of long-term processes such as distance and cutoff. "Cutoff is so prevalent among us that America has been called 'a nation of cutoffs.'" (Gilbert, 2004, 58).

Think of it. When your relatives left the old country to become immigrants in America, didn't they leave behind friends and family? Was it hard or impossible to keep in touch?

When they settled on the East Coast, did they eventually head west? Did they cut off from family and friends in the East? How many generations of cutoff has your family endured?

If we consider the future generations of our loved ones, our friends and neighbors, and our fellow citizens, what would happen if we shift from blame, avoidance, drama, control, or regret to understanding, the tenderness of empathy, or even love? From worry and fear to sincere interest and calm listening? From cutoff to reaching out, and rekindling connections?

My clients who become interested in the job of rekindling connections find that they frequently receive warm smiles and appreciation when they take the time to reach out. This is the beginning of overcoming cutoff. It isn't an easy or comfortable thing to do—but a worthwhile step.

If we want to reverse rather than increase generational and societal regression, one big question faces us: Do we pass on our own emotional immaturity, or can we grow our understanding, love, and virtue to be visited upon the generations to come?

Perhaps one thought can motivate us to act: The continuation of life on our Mother Earth could very well depend upon our choices.

. . . .

At a Glance: Thinking Big–The Seventh Generation Principle

- The Bowen theory and the Bible concur that weakness (or iniquity) patterns get passed on through the generations.
- It is also true that strengths get passed on and benefit many, as the appreciative quotes about George Washington indicate. Bowen theory observed that phenomenon as well.
- Bowen theory requires neither pushing nor forcing another to change. That would be an anxiety-binding process. Instead, Bowen theory only asks the motivated person to nudge themselves to change.
- The Haudenosaunee Iroquois Confederacy has had more years of success with their democracy than we have had to date with ours. It seems wise to consider emulating their dedication to decisions that benefit living beings and the earth for seven generations. There is no time like the present to also emulate their equality between the sexes.
- I respect and honor the example of democracy enjoyed by the Haudenosaunee Iroquois Confederacy, as well as the many who have sincerely worked to create and support democracy in any country.
- Any negative pattern can be changed today by someone making a conscious effort to reverse it. It is not easy, but it will benefit the pioneer who makes this effort as well as others in the family and the generations to come.

Practical Tips

1. Start by choosing one decision you are facing. Ask yourself: how would I ideally like this to affect my generation? The next? Begin by thinking of just two generations. As you gain comfort with that, start thinking of the effect on two generations from you.

Intensions are powerful. You are making definite progress in the direction of more conscious living.

2. Consider creating a family diagram of those who belong in your family. Start with at least three generations in your family, adding the birth year of each member (and deaths if relevant). As you read the book, you can add symbols for the relationship patterns each person practices. You will find instructions on how to create a family diagram at ibetherapy.com/relationshipresources.

Chapter 2
Using Desensitization to Wake Up Your Healthy Mind

"Both men and women should feel free to be sensitive. Both men and women should feel free to be strong. . . . It is time that we all perceive gender on a spectrum not as two opposing sets of ideas."

Emma Watson

"We often add to our pain and suffering by being overly sensitive, over-reacting to minor things, and sometimes taking things too personally."

Dalai Lama

"Manners are a sensitive awareness of the feelings of others."

Emily Post

A pop quiz will precede each discussion beginning with this chapter. Taking the quiz will help you to introspect before you are introduced to concepts which you may or may not find new or awkward. Please answer sincerely without concern about whether your answer is right or wrong. Whether it is true or false—for you, it is correct. You might return to the quiz after reading the chapter or book to see if your answers changed or remained the same. Appendix 2 provides a key with ideal answers based on Bowen theory.

Pop Quiz

T or F I've been emotionally triggered by someone's words, decisions, or behavior and couldn't get past it for a long time.

T or F I have the kind of sensitivity that allows me to feel compassionate and considerate of the feelings and needs of others.

T or F I often become so emotional I cannot think or reason clearly.

T or F I tend to get hurt and withdraw from people without warning.

T or F I don't like to think about how challenging it is for others to be close to me.

Desensitizing anxiety and stress

Desensitization means to become more calm and centered, and less swayed by negative self-talk and distressing emotions. According to the Cambridge English dictionary, it means causing "someone to experience something, usually an emotion or a pain, less strongly than before."

Despite the great value of desensitization, I had taken the concept for granted. It had never occurred to me to devote a whole chapter to it in this book. But a participant from my Integrative Bowen and EMDR (iBE) Workshop pointed out how key it is for people to understand the value of desensitization. She urged me to start my book with a chapter on this subject. She's right and I'm grateful to her. It is a vital subject.

One of the hidden things about us that we can be blind to, is just how sensitive we can be. This chapter introduces theory to help you understand the reasoning behind the practical advice you will learn throughout the book.

You can turn this chapter into practical help by keeping your journal nearby as you read. Note examples of sensitivity you relate to. Are there some sensitivities you would like to be free of? Or, have you been told it would be good if you were more sensitive?

Look for insights on just how healthy your mind can become, naturally and more rapidly than most believe possible. Many people spend years in talk therapy and find growth is slow.

Anxiety and stress are two aspects of life that, as members of a high-stress society, we often consider normal parts of life. We become so used to living life in fight or flight mode that we either don't notice we're stressed, or we come to accept it, thinking that everyone is like this.

During my career as a therapist, I was fortunate to discover two amazing healing approaches, both of which maximize desensitization. I've studied and used Bowen theory for thirty-five years. Its primary goals are to promote emotional maturity in order to decrease or desensitize anxiety. I found EMDR twenty years ago. It desensitizes emotional stress, helping the brain's natural health and strength bounce back.

In my work, I have combined the two modalities, calling the new approach Integrative Bowen and EMDR (iBE). The results have been amazing. The Bowen theory and EMDR therapy together help people clear blockages based on past experiences and more quickly integrate new strategies for change and growth.

For example, my clients don't need to come back to me for years. Many of them complete their therapy in an average of six months. They are making progress in relationships quicker than they or I could have imagined.

Bowen theory and EMDR therapy have a commonality: they want to help people who have stress and anxiety to reduce the stress and access their strengths. Both approaches want to desensitize anxiety.

In EMDR, the first emphasis is to become aware of your level of anxiety or distress, to understand how anxiety is related to unresolved memories, and to lower emotional distress through the EMDR therapy protocol.

Unknown to many of us, anxiety causes relationship issues. With Bowen theory, the emphasis is on becoming aware of the relationship consequences of your unconscious anxiety. Understanding the outcome of your actions is a strong motivator for you to overcome any anxiety and stress that are interfering with your success and happiness in life.

As EMDR developer Francine Shapiro's self-help book title implies, *Getting Past Your Past* is the goal of EMDR.

Reprocessing—EMDR's advantage

Shapiro originally called eye movement desensitization and reprocessing (EMDR) EMD (eye movement desensitization). She observed the steady and efficient desensitization of clients' negative, irrational self-beliefs. As time progressed, she was also thrilled to witness cognitive change and other positive shifts occurring spontaneously during EMD sessions.

Shapiro called this reprocessing (thus, her research report introduced the acronym EMDR). Shapiro thought of the brain as a computer processer. She used the term reprocessing to convey that the way the memory was stored became changed permanently following EMDR. It was as if the memory file was edited and saved with a positive conclusion about oneself.

Cognitive change means change in beliefs, such as moving spontaneously from, "I'm not good enough" to "I'm fine as I am."

As a result, EMDR was an improvement over cognitive behavior therapy, which requires hours of homework to achieve similarly successful outcomes. EMDR requires little to no homework. Both therapies have a success rate of at least 80 percent, reported by many quality research studies. This is the reason both are recommended by the World Health Organization for the treatment of PTSD.

It also became clear that EMDR was able to desensitize client's emotions of hurt, shame, frustration, grief, rage, despair, or disgust. The change was perceptible—decreasing from client ratings of eight, nine, or ten out of ten down to three, two, one, and often zero.

During EMDR, the client is asked to visualize a disturbing memory along with the negative belief, disturbing emotions, and sensations that go with the memory. The therapist guides the client to do eye movements while dwelling on the memory with all its aspects. Desensitization begins and continues.

What does desensitization look like?

When a memory is desensitized, the disturbing visual image of the memory begins to recede, getting further away, less vivid, or like a movie on a screen. This happens as the eye movements proceed in short periods, followed by breaks to notice how the client feels while attending to the issue.

The same EMDR process that results in emotional relief often desensitizes many physical sensations that accompany the client's emotion if they originated with the memory or soon after. For example, if physical sensations are tied to the unresolved memory, a tight chest, difficult breathing, feelings of nausea or disgust in the gut, deep pain or sadness in the heart, heavy shoulders, or back pain, these are often reduced or eliminated.

Even research on phantom limb pain treated with EMDR has demonstrated this treatment can reduce or eliminate continuing pain long after the injury and amputation occurred (Schneider et al., 2008).

The heart of EMDR

Desensitization is the heart of EMDR. It is the fourth phase of an eight-phase process. This phase involves using eye movements or other gentle, bilateral stimulation of the brain. The result of the bilateral stimulation is that distressing thoughts, memories, emotions, and sensations become less bothersome.

Other EMDR bilateral stimulation methods have been shown to be effective. These include tactile stimulation through tapping hands or knees, or using two pulsars held in the hands with the vibration alternating from one to the other. Audio stimulation can be offered through headphones programmed with alternating tones or music with a track that alternates sound from one ear to the other.

The purpose of bilateral stimulation is to stimulate the right and left brain hemispheres to help access dysfunctionally-stored information as well as adaptive information.

How our minds heal—adaptive information processing (AIP)

Dysfunctionally-stored information consists of memories stored in a highly-charged form. These include negative images, beliefs, emotions, and physical sensations. They feel true because of their strength. The memories can cause flashbacks, in which the past feels like it is happening in the present.

Adaptive information consists of positive memories and experiences that have provided positive self-concepts, emotions, images, and sensations. These feel true in a different way, due to a calm sense of conviction.

We have what Shapiro calls an adaptive information processing system (AIP). This system helps us shift how memories are stored. The AIP emerges naturally after desensitization. Shapiro (2012, 20) puts it this way:

> If we cut ourselves, unless there is an obstacle, we tend to heal. If we remove the block, the body goes back to healing. That's why we're willing to let ourselves be cut open during surgery. We expect incisions to heal.
>
> The brain is part of the body. In addition to the millions of memory networks . . . we all have hardwired into our brains a mechanism—an information processing system—for healing. It is geared to take any sort of emotional turmoil to a level of mental health or what I call a level of adaptive resolution. This means a resolution that includes the useful information that allows us to be more fit for survival in our lives. The information processing system is meant to make connections to what is useful, and let go of the rest.

The desensitization process can be emotional, but it is sometimes quieter. As one client reported with surprise about his silent experience: "I had no idea I didn't have to talk to heal! Sticking with it, letting go of words and thoughts—it opened me up to my Higher Power."

How Bowen desensitizes clients

Bowen also was concerned about the ways emotional reactivity can harm our thinking, choices, behavior, and our relationships. Emotional reactivity was Bowen's term for anxiety that affects our perceptions, physiology, and behavior.

Emotional reactivity is the outer expression of our inner sensitivity. It includes spontaneous negative responses such as expressions of anger, criticism, fear, sadness, or hurt.

Bowen therapists work toward desensitizing reactivity—even though they may not use that term. Bowen practitioners (or coaches as Bowen called them) use neurofeedback, deep breathing, and a broad Bowen perspective. They look for patterns that are present in families spanning generations. This assists their clients in becoming more neutral and less emotionally-reactive.

Neurofeedback has been proven to help people focus calmly. This, and simple deep breathing can accomplish the same goal. Both help people slow down the response time after something distressing has happened. The cost of neurofeedback is significant and is not always covered by insurance. However, deep breathing costs nothing but a little conscious thought. It brings in extra oxygen—a free, natural tranquilizer with no side effects.

Why desensitize?
Why is desensitization a practical and relevant goal for a healthier relationship? Why might you want to desensitize? Sensitivity is often a daily occurrence.

- We all have certain words, values, mannerisms, looks, or voice tones that can trigger us into emotional reactivity. Most people are sensitive to whining, grating, or irritated tones of voice. They feel accused, as if the words "you're wrong," were spoken.
  - This is because something in the past happened that was similar to the present behavior. The person on the receiving end is triggered in the present. It feels as if what happened before is happening again.
  - Our healthy AIP (adaptive information processing system) is there, but not actively working if too many unresolved negative memories are stored in the brain. This emotional overload makes it difficult to access our strengths, so we easily react in ways that can embarrass or disappoint us and others in our world.

- When you receive feedback that seems like criticism, do you think about it for days, find your heart pounding, or find it hard to sleep?
  - This could be a result of being exposed to criticism frequently in the past. It's as if you were hit again and again in the same place, which created a sore spot. The slightest touch of the spot creates a "Yow!" response. Even a hint at criticism might trigger a self-limiting belief such as, "I'm not good enough."
  - Or, perhaps you witnessed a family member or classroom peer being criticized. In the iBE workshops, people often choose to work on witnessing criticism. Through their empathy, they feel pain when they see loved ones in pain.
  - Perhaps the opposite is true. Maybe you never received objective negative feedback at home. Every act of yours was praised as if you could do no wrong. However, as you grew up, others didn't see you that way. Today do you feel uncomfortable when others don't like something you do? Is it at times intolerable? Do you want to find fault with them or dismiss them or their opinion? Does this ever end your relationships?
- Are you in a relationship with someone like this? Do you walk on eggshells around that person, whether at work or at home? Do people walk on eggshells around you? Under these conditions, people can push each other's buttons so easily that fights or breakups are potential dangers. Such people end up with small support systems (see chapter 4 for more about support systems).

Desensitization can greatly improve these common examples of discomfort or pain. Once a distressed memory is desensitized with EMDR therapy or another method, we can better access more of the strengths stored in our AIP. "Desensitization is so freeing!" said one iBE group participant.

As people desensitize their emotional reactions, they simultaneously make it easier to be emotionally-mature with others. It is as if a more complete library of their minds becomes available as an internal resource for addressing current challenges in relationships and in life.

Our senses can deceive us

Sensitivity is literally based on our senses, and our senses can deceive us. Anyone who has seen a mirage knows the truth of this.

Our senses get particularly warped, influenced, or distorted when we are stressed, anxious, or emotional. The stress hormones start to course through our bloodstream. At best, we become mildly vigilant. At worst, adrenaline triggers a hyper-vigilant reaction. We look for evidence of danger while ignoring evidence of well-being.

Although this heightened state of reactivity may seem normal because it's common, the good news is we do not have to live our lives this way. We are sensitized because of stresses or traumas specific to our own lives. These can originate from work deadlines, misunderstandings with people, accidents, illnesses, natural disasters, and other events.

The difficult experiences may have happened enough times that the child, teen, or young adult was unable to shake them off anymore. They happened too strongly or unexpectedly. The trigger brings the same response as it did in the past—a flooding of emotion.

When people accuse you of wanting to hurt, control, or manipulate them in some way, their words or expressions can come across as harsh. This can trigger sensitivity in you. For example:

- "The word you used hurt me."
- "When you didn't do what I thought you should do, I realized you don't care about me at all."
- "You always want me to be perfect!"

Example: a trip to the nursery

These common accusations and others like them can arouse emotional reactivity. One day at my favorite nursery as we were packing our mulch into the car, we couldn't help but overhear a man loudly accusing his wife, "Woman, are you stupid? Don't shove it in through the back window! Come here and put it in through the door."

She looked flustered and smiled to us in embarrassment as she rounded their car, getting closer to ours. That brought the man's attention to us, and he changed his entire demeanor. He flashed a big smile and with a kindly voice wished me "Happy Mother's Day."

The husband was reacting with emotional anxiety which he projected onto his wife. When he saw us, he collected himself to a degree.

I couldn't help but think that his sudden accusations gave his wife a feeling of dread for the drive home. We only knew that two-minute snippet of their day. Perhaps the husband was already sensitized by something that happened earlier.

Sensitivity can be positive or negative

When people are clueless about our goodwill, integrity, or love even after knowing us for some time, it is sad. We'd hoped they had paid attention and noticed the signs of our caring. It might occur to us: "I wish that person had more sensitivity to me—to my needs!" Gentle sensitivity, when present, can add grace to a relationship.

This brings light to the reality that sensitivity can be desirable in some forms, and problematic in other forms. When it contains consideration and empathy, it is a joy to be around. People who do this are said to be sensitive to others.

Most of us would not want to give up sensitivity altogether. Tender, gentle moments, touches, words, and glances enrich our lives and relationships. Sensitivity adds richness to life when people feel for others with the same care they feel for themselves. A whole-hearted interest in others enables us to understand them better, and even to lift them up when they are down.

Elizabeth, one of my clients, however, had so much sensitive empathy that it tortured her. She could cry for hours after hearing the news of someone who was suffering. Since she is committed to empathy as the most important quality, she accepts it as a necessity. Yet she regularly goes into suicidal depressions triggered by her empathy.

I offered Elizabeth a story to help her understand that even desirable qualities can be undesirable and dangerous when overdone.

Let's imagine that Jerry falls into a pit of quicksand. If due to her great empathy, Jerry's friend, Jenny jumps into the pit to have the same experience Jerry has, both will drown in the quicksand. The Bowen term for this kind of empathy is fusion—complete joining together.

But if, in Jenny's balanced empathy, she keeps herself safe and runs to find a safe way to rescue Jerry, she is making a proper use of empathy and protecting them both.

How EMDR therapy can help painful sensitivity

During desensitization in EMDR, the brain is helped to do accelerated processing of information. I call it emotional digestion, as do many EMDR therapists. In fact, in her 2007 book for children, *Dark, Bad Day . . . Go Away!*, Ana Gomez explains to children that "EMDR means eyes moving to digest and recover."

When we eat our food, we chew it, adding digestive enzymes to food in the mouth. The food moves down to the stomach, where hydrochloric acid and other juices further break it down.

In the intestines, the nutritional value of the food is extracted for the body's use. The waste products are moved out. If we eat way too much, we are in danger of a blockage. The blockage can cause pain as well as toxins that recycle in the body. Accumulations of toxins can cause disease.

Similarly, when we attempt to digest too many stressful experiences we can develop blockages. Our brains naturally use the REM (rapid eye movement) period of sleep to help memories digest. So, in a sense you have been desensitizing to some degree every day of your life. The eye movements compare to chewing food in our digestion metaphor.

Sleep research has demonstrated that if our REM sleep is regularly interrupted, we don't get to chew or process our experiences as thoroughly, and thus they don't fully digest. Our brains' natural self-healing capacity becomes overwhelmed.

This happens when we have high stress. We develop a pile-up in the brain much like blockages in the gut. In the gut, this would cause great pain. Such a pile-up of undigested experiences in the brain can cause emotional pain such as depression, anxiety, or post-traumatic stress disorder.

Robert Stickgold of Harvard has hypothesized that EMDR jump-starts again the healthy process that REM offers our brains to assist in the integration of new experiences (Stickgold, 2002).

Brain activity before and after desensitization

Figure 2.1, the brain scan of a woman who survived two violent physical attacks, shows a highly-sensitized, dramatically-activated brain. The bright red areas reveal significant electrical and blood flow activity. These areas are overworking, trying to manage the stress related to agitated memories.

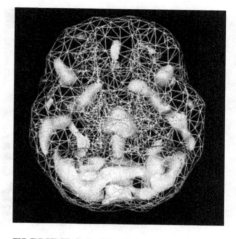

Dr. Daniel Amen, who took the SPECT scan of this woman, diagnosed her with PTSD. The EMDR therapist who treated her concurred.

FIGURE 2.1. Brain scan of attack survivor prior to EMDR

Scan by Dr. Daniel Amen

After a person has been desensitized through EMDR, she can experience the same outer triggers, such as driving in the same location, or seeing a person of the same build and appearance, without being triggered within. The person knows there is a difference between the present and the past. There is a sense of new lightness and freedom. They no longer need to live in dread of the trigger getting control of them again and again.

Figure 2.2 shows the new brain scan of the same woman after completing four, ninety-minute EMDR sessions.

The brain activity is significantly calmed. The bright red area at the lower right is the cerebellum. This area monitors the body's vital signs and needs to be on duty 24/7. It is ideal for this area to be active.

According to Amen, the small red dots toward the center of the brain show that she is experiencing a little depression, far less than in her original scan.

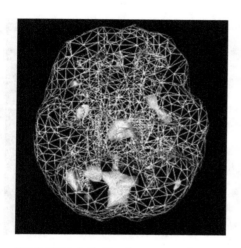

FIGURE 2.2. Brain scan of attack survivor following EMDR

Scan by Dr. Daniel Amen

This illustrates the value of desensitizing harmful aspects of sensitivity. This brain now has plenty of territory available for the AIP to activate.

Container exercise: self-help when your brain is sensitized

One valuable self-help method is the container exercise. It activates the talent of your creative, image-oriented, right brain hemisphere.

The right hemisphere thinks it is cool if you imagine a temporary holding tank, a container big enough and strong enough to hold any memories, issues or worries that are weighing upon you. Notice the color of your container. If it is a clear container, I ask that you be ready to cover it with a cloth. The container needs to have a secure method of being closed. Picture your container now as you put the book down and close your eyes.

Now you want to help the brain to take a break from its heavy load of worries or distress. Put the memories and emotions in your container, however you want to do that. Some people imagine the memories are on DVDs and put them in the container. Some imagine them as computer files. Others let the memories and feelings flow into the container like a grey cloud. If you are focusing on the individual memories and getting upset, shift to the grey cloud method.

When you feel that all or most of the distressing material is in your container, secure it shut. Now notice how you feel inside. Do you feel better? Where do you notice the nicer feeling? Put your hand on that location. Savor the feeling. Congratulate yourself that you have the ability to use imagination to help you.

Now imagine putting a sign on your container: "To be opened when it serves my healing."

Your brain will cooperate with the container exercise as long as you use the container as a temporary holding tank. If you use it as a place to bury your memories, your brain will not cooperate. It will eventually remind you of the distressing memories, sometimes when you least expect it.

The container exercise is good to use during times of transitions. I recommend practicing it three to five times a day. Good times would be at the close of the work day, after a stressful drive, and at the end of the day. The more you practice it, the more it can become a life-long resource. It is an exercise of setting boundaries with your own mind. If you make a little progress and your memories stay in the container for a little while, that is good.

If the memories pop out again, you can train them like you train a dog: "Go back."

If you find you need a little extra help, look for The Four Elements Exercise for Stress Management later in this chapter. Practicing the container followed by Four Elements can help you take some layers off of intense distress.

Angie's AIP

Angie is a young woman in her thirties. When she was four, her stressed mother (who never wanted children) effectively locked her in the bedroom by putting a child safety knob on her bedroom door knob. Angie's long-term negative belief was born at age four: "I'm not lovable." She spent her life striving to be the perfectly caring, available friend so she could be loved.

As Angie processed that intensely painful memory from age four, plus others showing her mother wanted to avoid her, she opened her eyes wide:

> Mom didn't live her life. She didn't feel. She wanted so much to be liked by her father, but it never happened. She turned that same aching heart to her husband, yearning for him to meet her needs. He was the one who wanted children. She had children to be loved by him. She didn't care about any of us kids. It is so sad.

When people reach the point of sincere compassion for the one who tormented them, it's often a sign that the distress is desensitized. I asked Angie, "What is the truest thing about you now?" She replied, "I am lovable, and Mom had problems."

What lies behind the AIP?

How could Angie's AIP be so talented as to suddenly know, "I am lovable" simply after desensitizing painful experiences that created the belief: "I'm unlovable?" The profoundness of being able to access something so positive in the midst of a painful life might come from a super-talented part of us—the intuition.

When a spontaneous, brand-new positive thought emerges out of the ashes of our lives, it is intuition, a spiritual quality, a knowing that comes from the soul.

I have witnessed people devise creative, positive solutions that fit their situation as the AIP is activating. The AIP includes the strengths gained from positive memories and calm reasoning ability. When activated, the ingenuity that often results is very inspiring to me.

The strengths gained from positive memories

Because Angie was able to shift her self-belief, Shapiro would predict that she had some former positive experience of being loved that taught her she was lovable. In fact, her father loved her a great deal. Angie had a positive memory her AIP could draw on.

The AIP is always present within. But it can be weighed down and inaccessible owing to a brain heavy with unresolved memories. Shapiro says at this point the processing is stuck and EMDR can jump-start it again.

Now Angie's memory is stored with the new realization that she herself is lovable even though her mother was incapable of loving. Her mother had such a wounded heart from her own unmet needs.

Think of how Angie could have been spared thirty years of pain if EMDR-AIP had been available to her mother to heal from the pain of having a dad who couldn't love. Think of how life could have gone if their marriage had been spared the pressures from her unmet needs of childhood.

The wonderful thing is, it is never too late to heal. I've worked with clients in their seventies and eighties. The AIP is alive and well, hidden inside them too. It just needs a little help to get out from the weight of the past.

Angie today

Angie is choosing EMDR to help dissolve thirty years of pain. She is still aware she experienced these events and feelings historically. But as we use iBE to process the themes of pain from her early life, her positive beliefs continue to strengthen.

She is able to transfer insights from the past into the present. She is now letting go of anxious overdoing for everyone who considers her their best friend. Her relationships in the past were not based on an equal give and receive.

Her pattern (Bowen's overfunctioning/underfunctioning reciprocity described in chapter 9) is in the process of change now. She is moving toward equality and balance in more of her relationships (see chapter 10, Choosing Balance and Equality).

Ana's happiness returns

Ana is in her fifties. She has spent decades in a very unhappy marriage, and months working for her divorce. The day after her divorce was granted in court, she said, "I've been away from happiness so long, and I am a doubter. How do I know that EMDR is working?"

I asked, "What have you noticed so far?"

She said, "I know I'm making progress because I feel lighter, happier, and more neutral. EMDR works silently and deeply. It bypasses my ever-so-active mental circus."

Yes, the AIP is alive after being well-hidden inside Ana, too. Now her natural happiness is returning.

Activate your own AIP

Start with a positive memory

Think of a time when you felt calm or confident. Allow yourself to mentally step into the memory. It may help to close your eyes. If so, you could ask a friend to read the instructions, or you could record the instructions for yourself.

Now that you have stepped into the memory, look around you. Notice the colors and shapes you see in the scene. Pay attention to the sounds you hear. Inhale. Notice the temperature of the air and the feeling of the air on your skin. Inhale again.

Do you catch any fragrance or aroma? Be aware of your body posture. Are you standing or sitting? Notice the points where your body is in touch with the earth or something else. Feel your body in the scene.

When you begin to notice a positive feeling inside, put your hand on the area where the feeling is strongest. Breathe and savor the feeling, like a wine connoisseur would savor a glass of fine wine.

An EMDR self-help method using tapping

Now, still enjoying the positive feeling, and keeping yourself in the scene, put your hands on your thighs, one on the left and one on the right, and slowly tap left, right, left, right to a total of two-to-six pairs of taps. When using a bilateral stimulation method (such as tapping) slowly and briefly, it has been found to enhance positive feelings and memories.

As long as the feelings are positive, you can practice this any time you want to be more calm or confident. Just like taking vitamins to boost your immune system, you can use this practice to boost your AIP.

Compare how you feel now to how you felt before the exercise. If you feel more calm or confident, this memory is a positive resource for you. It is part of your AIP. You can use it at other times in the future when you again want to feel more calm or confident. In fact, you will use it again in a moment.

If you do not feel better after dwelling on this memory, ask yourself if there was some negative association with the positive memory. If so, please choose another memory that is free of that issue and try the exercise again. If you still have difficulty, I suggest Francine Shapiro's very thorough self-help book, *Getting Past Your Past* for other ways to find positive resources to help you.

A self-help stress reduction exercise

Elan Shapiro, MA (2012) developed an exercise he called, "The Four Elements Exercise for Stress Reduction."

I adapted it by adding bilateral stimulation (pedaling the feet). Thanks to Elan Shapiro for permission to paraphrase his easy, effective method (below) to help you regain a feeling of safety and stabilization.

Each of the four elements listed is followed by the purpose of the exercise. Next, the instructions are provided. The way to focus your attention is defined in brackets.

Earth: Grounding, safety in the present. Notice your feet on the floor. Feel the floor and the chair supporting you. Feel the firmness of the floor and notice how it connects you to the ground below the building. Pedal your feet a little, left, right, left, right as you notice that now in this room you are safe, is that right? We would never waste the time to do this exercise if we weren't safe. And as you pedal, notice how stable the floor is. [Attention is directed outward to the reality of safety in the present.]

Air: Deep breathing for centering. Do deep abdominal breathing, expanding your abdomen as you inhale and pulling it in as you exhale. Continue for six to twelve breaths as I let you know what is happening. This is a powerful method to help you shift out of the fight or flight state. When we breathe rapidly and shallow, the body reads that as a signal that we need adrenalin. We get primitive, as if a saber tooth cat is coming around the corner. If that is not true, and we don't need to defend our lives, the adrenaline is not helpful. The sooner we can close the adrenaline valves pumping that powerful drug into our system, the better. The air step is potent, because it tells the body you don't need adrenalin. Also, it provides you with ample oxygen, a natural tranquilizer as mentioned previously. [Attention is directed inward to your center.]

Water: Becoming calmer and in control, to switch on the relaxation response. Do you have saliva in your mouth? Make more saliva by twirling your tongue in your mouth. I'll explain what is happening while you do that. When the fight or flight switch is turned on, the rest and digest switch is turned off. These are two mutually exclusive switches. Fight or flight only uses the systems that will help you survive. That includes your large muscles such as arms, legs, and heart. It includes your primitive, reptilian brain. But things that are non-essential for survival, such as the digestive system and complex thinking, are turned off during fight or flight. That way all the body's energy is used for the one purpose of survival. This is how adrenaline helps people run faster or enables a mother to be strong enough to lift a car off her child. All we need to do to switch fight or flight off and rest and digest on, is to swallow the saliva. [Attention is directed to producing saliva and becoming calmer, focused, and more in control.]

Fire: Light up your imagination while accessing a positive memory. "This is when you can bring up the memory you accessed a few moments ago. Once you can picture the memory and feel the good feeling in your body, tap left and right briefly and slowly." [Attention is directed to the feelings of calmness or confidence in your body.]

I educate clients that The Four Elements Exercise has the capacity to reduce your stress level by one or two steps (on a ten-point scale) each time you do it. However, if you practice it three to five times a day, before or after activities such as meals, the commute to work, waking or retiring at night, you will find you become more skilled. I have seen clients able to reduce stress by three points after a month of practice.

I believe this exercise is a good one to use throughout life. By being aware of your stress level, you can help yourself promptly when the stress level is mild or moderate. Thus, you can keep yourself in a window of tolerable emotion rather than in a high arousal state or a shut-down state.

Four Elements is a resource you can teach to receptive others. You might empower them to reduce their stress levels.

When feeling distress

You can also access a self-help EMDR method of alternatingly tapping your knees to help desensitize yourself when feeling distress. Do this for six to eight pairs of slow taps while breathing smoothly. While tapping, notice your feelings without judging them.

Take a deep breath and a break. See if you feel a little better. If so, add another set of taps (also six to eight pairs of taps), staying with your emotion.

After each set, take a deep breath and just notice how you feel now. If you continue to feel a little better, continue taps followed by breaks for up to five minutes. This will help you experience desensitization for yourself.

Cautionary note:

Tapping too much or too fast can open your mental box of memories and you could find a surprise package of a very painful memory. It is hard to predict who this could happen to. Even highly competent professional counselors have experienced this.

Therefore, please follow the guidelines offered. It is easy to get excited about positive results and think that more would be better. Experience has taught us that is not the case. It is better to be content with good results.

Maintaining positive sensitivity

As previously mentioned, sensitivity has many positive aspects.

With EMDR Therapy we need not worry about giving up positive sensitivity. The desensitization phase of EMDR is guided by the health and intelligence within your brain's AIP system. I tell clients, "Your brain will be the star of this show."

Magically, the bilateral stimulation used during the desensitization phase of EMDR desensitizes negativity, but not positivity. Here is a fascinating example:

Heather came to me for help after she survived an airplane crash due to the outstanding efforts of the pilot. He made a safe emergency landing in a field. There were injuries, but no deaths. In our sessions, we used EMDR therapy to desensitize all her negative images, thoughts, feelings, and sensations surrounding the emergency landing. She was progressing well.

Then suddenly she had a vivid memory of the kind man who ran across the field and came directly to her to help. He attended to Heather with welcomed sensitivity and kindness. I said, "OK, notice that," and began to guide her to do more eye movements.

"Oh, NO! I don't want to erase that!" Heather exclaimed.

It was as if she thought my hand movements to guide her eye movements were a giant eraser, because the distress associated with her memories seemed to be getting erased.

"Don't worry," I assured her. "Your brain knows what's worth dumping and what's worth keeping. Your healthy AIP system will make those decisions. I think you will find your AIP really wants you to remember this man."

She allowed me to proceed with the eye movements. Heather found that this memory remained intact and she continued to enjoy it.

Secondary traumatization

In a different example where negativity was desensitized while allowing positivity to strengthen, let us turn to Corrine's story. Her husband Ron faced a frightfully aggressive case of cancer. At one point a feeding tube was recommended. He fiercely resisted it, but after severe weight loss, he agreed.

When he passed out right after a feeding, Corrine was alarmed. He soon came to, got up, stumbled, and accidentally pulled the tube out of his stomach! She got him to the ER, while he protested all the way.

Fortunately, Ron became completely free of cancer within twelve months of diagnosis. Corrine's sensitivity to Ron's needs was an important factor in his healing process. It graced a deepening bond between them.

But shortly after he was cleared of cancer, capable Corrine started to have PTSD symptoms. She had flashbacks, panic attacks, sleeping problems, and became highly anxious at work where she began having memory problems (a common PTSD symptom).

It was as if she had put all her needs on hold, considering his needs to be uppermost. She was acutely sensitive to all that was needed to promote his survival. This was too all-consuming for her to be able to attend to her own needs.

Intensely anxious sensitivity began popping up for her without warning. It was a totally unwelcome sensitivity. Her savvy nurse practitioner referred her to me for EMDR therapy.

This kind of secondary traumatization happens frequently for loved ones. I've assisted parents whose children have endured grave medical conditions. The parents managed amazingly well until the children were free of the illness, even though the illnesses lasted up to two or three years.

At that point, the parents' symptoms began to feel crazy, unrelated to their current life. That is exactly true. The symptoms were all related to the past trauma empathetically witnessed for their little loved one. The parents' stress or trauma was stored in the brain in a relatively raw form.

PTSD from primary traumatization and secondary traumatization are stored in the brain in the same way. The stresses come from direct experience or witnessed experience, but cause the same symptoms. These symptoms are well-known in PTSD, but they are also found in people with secondary traumatization.

The politics of PTSD

Many people think PTSD requires some extreme event such as war or rape or being in a life-threatening accident. While those things of course can cause PTSD, Scott et al. reported in the 1994 *British Journal of Psychiatry* that non-life-threatening stressors can also result in significant PTSD scores.

The big question is, why? Well, let's look at what can cause PTSD: a bad breakup, a nasty divorce, a set-back at work, witnessing something distressing happening to a loved one or even a stranger on the street, being shunned or bullied at school or work, having a broken bone (the PTSD rate for fractures is 54 percent), or a cancer diagnosis in yourself or a loved one. All kinds of distressing events can result in symptoms of PTSD.

The cause of PTSD has become a controversial issue, because PTSD is the only diagnosis therapists identify as requiring a particular kind of experience. Since 1980 when the name post-traumatic stress disorder was first identified, the PTSD diagnosis has required a life-threatening event.

Many trauma therapists know about Scott's research, but what is more important—their own clinical work confirms his conclusions. Hopefully the American Psychiatric Association's *Diagnostic and Statistical Manual of Mental Disorders* will soon be more closely aligned with the experience of clients and therapists.

It is unfortunate that the original impressions dating back to 1980 continue to determine this diagnosis. I believe the current standard does a great disservice to the public, because most people who have PTSD have no idea they could have it.

They are aware they are terribly nervous, anxious, and/or depressed. But many have expressed, "PTSD is something drastic and extreme, and only applies to war combat veterans." This is a partially true (it does apply to war combat veterans). Because of this, a false prejudice is easily spread by news reports of soldiers having PTSD, while few other examples of the condition are reported.

People either don't feel worthy to have PTSD or they discourage others from getting help for it. Surprisingly, Corrine's mother told her she shouldn't make light of a war veteran's PTSD by saying she had it herself.

Despite the prejudice about PTSD, many people are highly sensitized by the symptoms of post-traumatic stress. These symptoms include: intrusive thoughts, nightmares and other sleep disturbances, flashbacks to negative events, persistent physical sensations for which doctors cannot find a cause, panic that doesn't seem related to anything happening in the present.

Unaware of PTSD, victims continue to suffer, often for many years longer than the originating event(s). In my experience, panic generally comes from untreated or insufficiently-treated past stress or trauma.

Corrine's first PTSD symptom was panic

Corrine is one example of someone suffering from PTSD who didn't realize it. Her situation started with panic at work. She had a highly responsible position in a finance corporation and had always felt very competent because she was careful and accurate with her numbers.

However, she began to make mistakes that caused losses for her company. This didn't make sense to her, and it terrified her. She started doubting her own mind. Soon she received two warnings that she could lose her job.

Had brain scans been used to diagnose Corrine, her brain would likely have looked very similar to the PTSD brain scan presented earlier in the chapter. But this wasn't necessary; her own symptoms provided the evidence.

Corrine's accumulated raw memories were taking over some of the territory for her short-term memory. I explained to Corrine that her memory problems might resolve by using EMDR to desensitize, process, and emotionally digest her distressing experiences.

This gave her hope, and she agreed to the EMDR Therapy. As we made progress applying EMDR, addressing a few memories of Ron's difficulties, she exclaimed, "EMDR is more potent than drugs!" She felt such relief with each memory processed. With sparkling eyes, Corrine said she could see herself becoming a healthy, happy person again.

Corrine's memory regarding the feeding tube was the fifth trauma we addressed using EMDR. Her husband's tube had pulled out and then slipped back in. On the day of the incident, she had googled the problem and learned about some of the complications that can result from a feeding tube forcefully coming out.

Ron had been upset with her because she insisted on taking him to the ER when he wanted to stay home. He grumbled about it. The medical people conducted many tests and found that he was fine, and that no injury or problem existed. It had taken many frustrating hours to receive that result.

I added Bowen principles into her EMDR session to assist her with any resulting relationship challenges. We particularly talked about the way she took an "I" position (see chapter 11).

Corrine shared a very interesting conclusion after completing the iBE work about the feeding tube. "If Ron gets upset with me, I don't have to take it so personally. My habit is to take things personally." What a healthy way to express the value of desensitization!

Corrine had experienced a painful aspect of sensitivity. She was only able to see it clearly the moment she became less sensitive.

She continued:

> When I took it personally, I didn't understand that his chief frustration was with the illness. His conflict wasn't with me, really. In general, I need to take things less to heart. It's OK if someone doesn't understand me and my motives. I don't want to judge them because they don't understand me. I did the right thing! Even though Ron was upset, and I thought he was upset with me, it was much more than me that irritated him.

This broad and objective view that Corrine reached came courtesy of the natural health of her brain, her AIP. I didn't suggest any of these ideas to her.

A couple of weeks later, Corrine reported an extra bonus: strangers were now approaching her in friendly ways naturally. She said that had never happened to her before. In my view, this is another reflection of the re-awakening of her AIP. In general, Corrine was more alive. People could feel it!

More potent than drugs

Corrine made an interesting pronouncement when she said, "EMDR is more potent than drugs!" In some cases, drugs may not be very potent. Many of my clients complain that psychotropic drugs either don't work or make them feel uncaring or even stupid. Of course, they can be life-saving as well.

A 2007 research study by Bessel van der Kolk et al. demonstrated that EMDR worked better than fluoxetine (Prozac) for PTSD.

For those curious to learn more about research on psychotropic drugs, please visit ibetherapy.com/relationshipresources. You'll find there a significant study there of the long-term effects of psychotropic medications on veterans. Additionally, you'll find meta-analyses of anti-depressant research that show that they work for severe depression, but not better than placebo for mild or moderate depression.

A milder example than PTSD

Professionals, businesspeople, and tradespeople often experience work-related challenges. These can concern relationships with a boss, coworker, or an employee. Or, it could be a frustration with oneself.

A common challenge for professionals and businesspeople is procrastination.

This might be related to moving forward in marketing their practice or business for example. This is completely understandable, as many have not been prepared for all the business skills for success. Marketing is a completely separate skill set. No wonder these people procrastinate, get sensitive, and in time feel like failures.

Dean was one of those. He was a psychotherapist in private practice who loved his work. He wanted the freedom to be his own boss and enjoy his family life. He launched his private practice with an excellent outreach to four hundred people. His schedule filled up and he felt great.

But in time his schedule developed openings. He worried about this and knew he should do more marketing. But he didn't know what to do. He thought the word of mouth by satisfied clients would do the marketing for him. He didn't speak with anyone about this. When his business wasn't bringing him the necessary income, he did the easy thing. He got a job where clients were provided for him.

However, he felt like a failure as the months passed. He worked a schedule that kept him from spending time with his family. He lost faith in himself. Finally he confided the situation to a good friend who insisted he try EMDR.

His EMDR therapy helped him quickly desensitize his memories of failure, including his negative feelings and beliefs. Then it dawned on him he needed to learn more skills. He turned to the Small Business Administration's SCORE program (previously known as the Service Corps of Retired Executives). Counselors were available to advise him about marketing strategies for free. He signed up for reasonably-priced courses. The first was to create a business plan. The second addressed internet marketing.

Dean surprised himself. He was eager to put his marketing knowledge into practice. He opened a part-time private practice. When it was full enough to replace the income from his job, he gave notice to his boss that he would be leaving.

Now he has a full-time practice. He's succeeded in his private practice by maintaining a routine of marketing and outreach.

Focusing on progress can help with sensitivity. Murray Bowen wanted to help people be less sensitive, in the sense of less emotionally-reactive to the distress around them. He worked toward this end from the 1950s to his passing in 1990. He coached people to pay attention to their progress and strive for objectivity, adopting the mindset of a researcher in their approach to their own lives.

This is a worthy effort which tends to help motivated people move forward in their desired direction. The downside is that it requires a patient, disciplined and often difficult effort, bringing progress slowly, usually in one to two or more years.

Bowen had a very positive, patient attitude about this. He said that even microscopic progress is huge. It is especially huge when a person is reversing a relationship pattern. People who reverse a relationship pattern such as conflict (see chapter 3), become resources for other struggling people. Bowen helped people focus on their progress while using breathing techniques to calm their sensitivity.

How Bowen and EMDR (iBE) calm emotional reactivity

EMDR works effectively with themes of distress. When something happens not just once, but repeatedly through our lives, do we have to address every single instance with EMDR? Thankfully, Shapiro discovered this isn't necessary.

Our brains have the capacity to generalize. While addressing just one instance is not quite sufficient, addressing three instances works wonders. We need to address:

1. The first memory of the repeated theme that is still disturbing
2. The worst memory

3. The most recent disturbing incident of this theme

To create a thorough and long-lasting result, I combined the above three types of memories with the four Bowen anxiety-binding categories. This is structured into iBE individual therapy as well as iBE group therapy. Note: Significant traumas should not be addressed in a self-help format. I want you to understand how the iBE therapy is structured.

Significant stress and trauma

I believe you can make a lot of progress through a self-help format or I would not have devoted years writing this book for you. However, if at any time you find your stress and anxiety so great that you need a breakthrough before you are ready to continue on your own, you may want to pursue one of the following:

1. EMDR therapy with an EMDRIA-certified EMDR therapist. I suggest two to four sessions concerning a single distressing event or issue.
2. Work with a Bowen coach regarding a frustrating relationship challenge that hasn't resolved through the self-help route (please do not give up on the complex people unless they are unsafe).
3. Or, an iBE therapist for either purpose. (I am still preparing an advanced iBE training for EMDR therapists. It should be available by late 2018 or 2019.)

Information for finding these resources is available at ibetherapy.com/relationshipresources.

Additionally, I encourage people who have experienced significant early negative experiences to do more than a few sessions. One way to judge the need is to take the Adverse Childhood Experiences Survey (ACES). You can access it through ibetherapy.com/relationshipresources.

If your ACE score is four or more (out of ten), I encourage you to get the EMDR help that can make a significant difference in your life. You will still benefit from this book and will likely find you need fewer sessions because of it. When I work with clients who have done their own self-help work first, I can tell because their healing work proceeds with a natural ease and efficiency.

What is next?

Are you ready to work on the universally-shared, challenging relationship patterns you might be using subconsciously? These repeating patterns do a good job of pushing whatever sensitive buttons your friends and family have. And when the patterns are brought to play by your friends and family in return, they can activate the lingering sensitivity responses you have that are always waiting in the wings for their entrance, until you desensitize them.

. . . .

At a Glance: Using Desensitization to Wake Up Your Healthy Mind

- To desensitize means to become more calm, centered, and less swayed by negative self-talk and distressing emotions.
- We consider anxiety and stress normal because it is so common, but our lives don't need to be so stressed.
- Bowen theory and EMDR therapy have a commonality: they want to help people with stress and anxiety.
- Chronic, subtle anxiety worsens relationship issues.
- In EMDR the emphasis is on becoming aware of the level of anxiety and lowering it through the desensitization stage of the EMDR protocol.

- With Bowen theory, the emphasis is on becoming aware of the relationship consequences of unconscious anxiety. This can strongly motivate you to overcome the anxiety.
- Reprocessing (the R in EMDR) means that our negative beliefs, once desensitized, are stored in a new, positive format.
- Our brains' adaptive information processing (AIP) systems naturally emerge following desensitization to store positive memories and experiences.
- When we have distressed memories, they manifest as highly activated areas in a brain scan.
- If our distress is triggered, we can use self-help methods including the container exercise, The Four Element exercise, and bilateral tapping to temporarily reduce distress and help us to feel more in control.
- PTSD can result from many kinds of stress or trauma; it is not limited to war combat veterans.
- Post-traumatic growth is a result of healing oneself from stressful memories.
- We don't have to desensitize every single memory related to a common distress to desensitize successfully—just the first, worst, and most recent.

Practical Tips

1. If you find yourself depressed or distressed, angry or ashamed, upset or confused use the container exercise to give yourself a mental vacation from the problem. Follow this up with The Four Elements Exercise.
2. When you are more calm, address what is distressing you by talking to someone you trust most or writing in a journal as if it is a letter to that person. Like a neutral reporter, describe exactly what happened. Then list all the feelings you have. Identify what you want, what is

most important to you. Close your eyes and lie back. Notice if you are feeling less sensitive, less emotional, more neutral.

3. Affirm: Even microscopic progress is huge. See if you can make a little progress by taking a positive step toward a solution.

4. Use other EMDR self-help techniques, including recalling a calm or confident memory to activate your AIP, and slow and brief bilateral tapping to enhance positive feelings and memories.

Chapter 3
Understanding Conflict

"Therefore all things whatsoever ye would that men should do to you, do ye even so to them." [For more examples of the Golden Rule, see appendix 3.]

Matthew 7:12

"Speak not injurious Words neither in Jest or Earnest. Scoff at none although they give Occasion."

65th Rule of Civility, George Washington

Mahatma Gandhi based his non-violent movement on the Hindu principle of ahimsa, as described in the Mahabharata scripture. However, Buddhist and Jain traditions practice ahimsa as well. Ahimsa (nonviolence) is defined as: The avoidance of harm to any living creature in thought or deed.

Pop Quiz

T or F I have felt battered by cruel or critical words.

T or F Others have been forceful with me physically and I don't like it.

T or F I really appreciate bossy and controlling people.

T or F Conflict has caused me to leave a relationship (T/F), a job (T/F), a school (T/F).

T or F I was completely blamed for a problem by a family member. It still bothers me.

Bowen on conflict

Bowen studied families that agreed to live in the hospital for observation of their behavior patterns. They hoped this could help their family member diagnosed with schizophrenia.

The first goal was to observe how families handled stress. Bowen hoped the results would be universal and not unique to these particular families. He called the patterns he discovered in their behavior anxiety-binding mechanisms (ABMs).

The first ABM Bowen's staff of researchers noticed was one any kindergartner might have volunteered: when people are upset, they fight. Bowen called this conflict.

Conflict includes everything from nit-picky criticisms to arguments with blame, accusation, judgment, or efforts to control. Sometimes conflict turns into a yelling match. On occasion, with some, it turns into violence.

My yoga teacher Johanna Torres chimed in on this theme: "The more force and aggression you put into anything, the faster you destroy it [your body, relationships, your marriage, your car]."

The ultimate extreme of conflict would be murder—complete disregard for the life of the other. Multiply individual conflicts, add "homies," and murder and you have gang violence. Keep multiplying the numbers and war becomes the most extreme form of conflict.

"My first wish is to see this plague of mankind, war, banished from the earth." [George Washington]

The dimensions of conflict

Isn't it true that we may fight or practice conflict with ourselves or with others, criticize ourselves or others, blame ourselves or others? No matter who is the target, we are involved in some form of conflict.

Conflict multiplies problems. If we aim conflict at ourselves, we will get depressed. If we aim it at others we may reap bigger retaliation. Or someone may stay with us only out of fear. Or they may become eager to give up and get away from us. Conflict can hurt the one who does it and the one who receives it.

I admit it. Conflict is my go to anxiety-binding mechanism. How could that be in a basically calm and harmonious person?

There are several reasons, but for now, a key one is that with my trained reluctance to talk about emotions (Mom said this was due to being Norwegian), and my inherent shyness, I had to get pretty emotional before I'd express anything. By that time, I was angry.

My milder and more honest hurt, or sadness, or disappointment never got air time. It was such a relief to get something out, that my inclination to release anger was rewarded and strengthened. In chapter 4 you'll see how I made progress in weakening that habit.

Sadly, conflict is a part of life

At home conflict affects marriages, siblings, parent-child relationships, and health. The effect can be mild, moderate, or extreme. Domestic violence is an extreme form, but less rare than you may think. Forty million of today's adult Americans grew up living with domestic violence. Fifteen million US children have observed domestic violence (2015, Childhood Domestic Violence Assn.).

At school, conflict affects peer relationships, teacher-student relationships. Increasingly it affects parent-teacher relationships and teacher-administration relationships. As a therapist, I have a lot of evidence for this.

Bullying has become so prevalent that 90 percent of fourth to eighth graders reported being victims of bullying (2010, Bullying Statistics.org).

At the workplace conflict affects relationships between peers, and between boss and employee. Managers report that 30 to 42 percent of their time is spent reaching agreement with others when conflicts occur (1996, Watson and Hoffman).

Conflict affects children at school, at home, and through cyber bullying. Cyber bullying can be considered conflict complicated by triangling on a massive level. Triangling is addressed in chapter 7. To describe it simply, triangling means bringing a third person (or more) into a problem. In cyber bullying, hundreds to thousands are, one-by-one, drawn into the fray.

Increasingly intense conflict permeates our entertainment media.

The effects of extreme conflict
Child abuse and domestic violence harms children and significantly interferes with maturation. Conflictual environments can affect physical and psychological health negatively.

Though most people consider physical abuse as more damaging than emotional abuse, the ACES (adverse childhood experiences) study of 17,000 Kaiser patients revealed that verbal/emotional abuse is the most harmful form (Felitti, 1998).

This is not to minimize the harm of physical or sexual abuse. Unfortunately, those abuses are often complicated by emotional abuse, which makes the harm sink in deeper. It can result in a diagnosis of complex trauma.

After studying verbal abuse by peers of young people, Teicher et al. in their 2010 article, "Hurtful Words: Association of Exposure to Peer Verbal Abuse with Elevated Psychiatric Symptom Scores and Corpus Callosum Abnormalities" concluded:

These findings parallel results of previous reports of psychopathology associated with childhood exposure to parental verbal abuse and support the hypothesis that exposure to peer verbal abuse is an aversive stimulus associated with greater symptom ratings and meaningful alterations in brain structure, specifically in the corpus collosum and corona radiata.

The corpus callosum is the major highway of fibers in the brain. It links the left and right hemispheres of the cerebral cortex.

The corona radiata is the highway of fibers linking the cortex to the brain stem.

Conflict doesn't just hurt our feelings. It hurts our brains.

Understanding conflict can lead to resolution

From a Bowen point of view, conflict is a symptom that can appear in any twosome.

It can occur in alternating cycles with emotional distance, or it can stand alone. . . . Each person focuses intently on what he/she believes the other to be doing wrong, ... The basic dependency between people is most clearly seen in conflict. Each tells the other clearly and forcefully how he/she has violated the dependence and what needs to be done to correct the situation. (Daniel Papero, 2017)

Educating ourselves about the dangers of conflict in all its facets can help motivate us to resolve the past and learn new adaptive ways for the future.

The goal of a Bowen approach to conflict is primarily for clients to learn facts about their role in conflict. Do I initiate conflict? When am I most likely to do so? Do I fan the flames? When is that most likely? When others initiate conflict, how do I respond next? Are there people whose conflict I can tolerate?

Who are they? What makes it easier with them? Are there those I cannot tolerate? What, exactly, is intolerable?

The role of the therapist or other helpful person is to be conscious of the degree to which he or she adds to the anxiety in the room or calms it. The hope is to maintain a calm environment in which maximum learning becomes possible. Yet, Bowen said all we need do to be effective is to be calmer than the other person. We don't need to attain some lofty level of perfect calmness.

Beyond personal conflict: the war between the sexes

Using calm, conscious thought to guide your actions is a powerful way to improve any relationship. When I was a new graduate student of Bowen theory, I learned about assertiveness as an effective way to deal with aggressive or disrespectful words. I was receiving cat calls and other comments from men during my walk home from the city bus stop after my night classes.

A friend had referred me to Rollo May's book, *Power and Innocence*. May hypothesized people use the highest level of power available to them. He ranked five types of power from strongest to weakest: Power of being (from prayer or meditation); self-affirmation (positive "I" statements to yourself); self-assertion (using "I" statements to speak up for yourself); aggression (often with "you" statements); and violence.

I was getting these comments regularly, and they made me feel increasingly uncomfortable. At first I tried ignoring them, but they didn't stop, and I found myself taking the tension and anger into myself.

Next I tried responding to their comments with anger. But I felt like I was adding to the war between the sexes and I realized they might pass my anger on to the next woman they saw. I also saw I was embracing Rollo May's description of aggression, low on the power scale.

I opted for one higher level on May's scale—self-assertion. I decided the next time to use very calm eye contact and a very short "I" statement. I felt like I had crested Mount Everest when my plan worked.

A group of men were harassing me from their car at an intersection. Instead of riling them to anger as my angry statements had done, I stooped to eye level with them in their car and calmly said, "I don't like being yelled at from the street." Their reaction was priceless. Their eyes widened, mouths dropped open, and they were frozen speechless.

The language of assertiveness was foreign to my perpetrators. Aggression was their highest level of power. It wasn't very powerful when addressed with calm, thoughtful assertiveness. I proved Rollo May was right.

Bowen's conflict training brought more progress

Bowen found that emotionally-mature people have somehow learned the lessons required to ease conflict, perhaps as painfully as I did, but maybe not.

They take "I" positions when their principles are at stake or they feel something is very important. They don't care much if others agree with them or not. They honor their own well-reasoned opinion, or thoroughly-felt emotion or values.

We'll learn more about "I" positions in chapter 11.

I find it very helpful to see conflict or aggression from the Bowen lens. Knowing these issues arise from anxiety and fear is revolutionary. Knowing that violent, aggressive people don't have higher forms of power leads me to feel a measure more of compassion, resulting in less judgment.

Gandhi's definition of ahimsa, or non-violence, helps expand the idea of harmful words and deeds to the realm of thought. To him, ahimsa is, "The avoidance of harm to any living creature in thought or deed."

Inner conflict

Do you ever find yourself becoming self-critical in a cruel rather than constructive way? This aspect of conflict blocks your success.

When you become an inner critic, you are your own worst enemy. This is a sad state of affairs. In the next chapter, the discussion of Bowen's study of emotionally-mature people provides steps to help with your inner critic. The bibliography lists books on this topic you may find valuable.

Conflict aimed at strangers

I was fortunate to come from a harmonious, fairly positive family, enjoying long periods of low stress. We didn't criticize a lot at home or with friends and loved ones. But, characters on TV, or strangers on the road were somehow fair game.

My dad only lost his temper with "jerks" on the road. I found his anger so out of character for him that my chief goal was to stifle my nervous laughter about this super-strange sight.

Interestingly, his habit, or anxiety-binding mechanism, was contagious. I developed an inner habit of criticizing people, usually strangers. It took me about ten years to become engrained in the habit, enough to be noticed by a highly intuitive person. He spontaneously gave me constructive feedback in just three short words: "Be fanatically positive."

"Wow! I'm caught," I thought.

But his guidance worked! In exchange for a negative thought, I created a positive replacement. For example, instead of, "I could never be happy dwelling so much on making my body perfect, like that woman," I thought, "Look at her joy in accomplishing her fitness goals."

I was learning to think more gently about others.

Do you find it entertaining to make barbs in jest, as Washington prohibited? Sarcasm is socially in vogue, but that doesn't make it harmless. Cruel words hurt. The hurt is multiplied when another is laughing while the person who is the butt of the joke is in pain.

To say, "I'm just joking" does not make it a joke. When someone has to say, "I'm just joking," it's a neon sign that he failed to be funny.

Meeting conflict with wise differing

Bowen theory lists anxiety-binding mechanisms (ABM). He shared lessons from emotionally mature people I have called maturity-building principles (MBP). I created a middle zone in between these two principles that is not in Bowen theory. I call this category wise protective patterns. To download a chart listing all three categories on a handy brochure, please visit ibetherapy.com/resources and click on the Bowen brochure pages.

The wise protective patterns may at first glance seem to be negative. They are simply thoughtful forms of the ABMs used in response to real threats. They are:

- Wise Conflict/Differing
- Wise Distance
- Wise Triangling
- Wise Overfunctioning/Underfunctioning Reciprocity.

I identified these patterns so people can get beyond the impression that patterns such as conflict, or war, are always bad. That view is too simplistic.

These strategies have evolved for social interaction out of necessity—just as fight or flight instincts evolved for basic survival against a predator set on eating us for lunch, or a dictator set on dominating the world.

ABMs are entered automatically with minimal conscious thought, like a knee-jerk response. No calm review of options precedes their onset. Also missing is introspection about one's various feelings concerning the perceived threat. In the case of ABMs, no one asks the basic question: "Is this threat real, or am I imagining it?"

But in the case of wise protective patterns, the functions missing from anxiety-binding mechanisms are present. Introspection happens, to determine the real complexities of the situation, followed by a rational review of options.

Let's look at what could be considered a wise use of what I call differing. Differing means to be unlike or dissimilar. Conflict is generally about differences. People have differing opinions, feelings, values, beliefs, goals, motives, and so on. When a person encounters differences with another, it often causes discomfort, and results in a jockeying to make one person right and the other wrong.

Looking at history, it is quite clear to most of the world that entering World War II was necessary for the allies to stop a dictator who was determined to wipe out the Jewish race in the name of ethnic cleansing, stealing art belonging to the Jews, taking over countries, and doing anything he could to magnify his own ego and race. Hitler's goals made him a danger to humanity.

It is wise and necessary to stop any harmful force that cannot listen to diplomacy to reverse its destructive ways. Stopping that force serves the greater good. We honor the leaders and soldiers who fought for that righteous cause and consider them heroes.

The difference between conflict used as an anxiety-binding mechanism and conflict used wisely involves the depth and quality of conscious, introspective thought and feeling that are applied to find solutions.

Wisdom consciously explores a complex reality until a virtuous path, or at least the next good step for action, becomes clear. Depth requires calmness to look thoroughly and long at the complex factors involved. Quality introspection is served by looking at the motives of oneself and others involved.

This is what the allies did. They pooled together their resources and talents and worked hard for the freedom of all.

. . . .

Wise conflict may be necessary when someone needs and wants protection. Words may be sufficient, or physical methods of defense or blocking attack may be called for. Self-defense, or defense of someone weaker, whether a child, an elder, or someone who doesn't know how to defend themselves, can keep an aggression from being completed.

I recommend self-defense for all in the spirit of wise protection. Parents who want to prepare their child for life would do well do consider finding a trustworthy teacher of either a martial art or an effective self-defense course. I recommend both courses.

The martial arts offer outstanding body discipline which can enhance one's mental discipline as well as self-control for any other sport, and for life. The self-defense course ensures that real situations are addressed practically and effectively.

Wise differing is a common element in the practice of the "I" positions Bowen learned about from his emotionally-mature subjects. To learn more about "I" positions, turn to chapter 11.

Violence increases along with appetite for conflict

Murray Bowen had concerns about the degree of cutoff in our culture. Cutoff is an extreme form of distance. Many of our ancestors left the old country to come to America. They did so at a time when communication was difficult.

Cutoff weakens relationships and can make individuals vulnerable to dysfunction. So, our nation began with a certain degree of cutoff affecting many immigrants. It is possible that our cutoff made us more vulnerable to conflict.

In "We Could Have Been Canada," Adam Gopnik in the May 15, 2017 issue of *New Yorker*, gives an added viewpoint. He observes that Americans embraced conflict to solve problems.

He makes the case that in separating from Britain, America is the only nation who did so with violence, rather than based solely on principles of democracy as we have been taught in our history classes.

Other historians are beginning to view history through this added lens of violence rather than solely through the lens of the principles we often point to as the founders' guiding lights.

While mulling over this issue, I chanced to hear National Public Radio's Robert Siegel, host of *All Things Considered*, interviewing Bob Ryan of the *Boston Globe*. The interview indicates our society is developing a tolerance for more conflict. Though it is not referring to the extreme of war, it concerns me nonetheless.

After the interview covered highlights of the previous thirty years, Siegel and Ryan discussed the difference in sports news coverage today versus thirty years ago:

> SIEGEL: *The Sports Reporters* show is unique on ESPN. Do you think it would be harder today to pitch a

show where four people talk intelligently and, you know, not always shouting about sports? Is that considered just not an apt idea anymore?

RYAN: What is not considered an apt idea is agreement. What is considered an apt idea is conflict. We weren't in it to seek conflict. If we had differing opinions, wonderful. It was organic. That was fine. But I have to tell you, and I'm a part of another program on the network, that sometimes we do manufacture issues for the sake of entertainment. And I don't think for one second we ever thought that way on *The Sports Reporters*.

SIEGEL: By the way, why was *The Sports Reporters* canceled? Was it expensive to bring everybody up to Connecticut every week to do, or just low ratings? Or what did they tell you?

RYAN: The only reason we were given—and I am not making this up, and I'm not being hyperbolic, I'm being—quoting verbatim—"We're going in another direction," unquote, unquote. So, you can take a look at the drift of the nature of some of the programs on the network now; it will tell you what direction that is in.

I wonder if the early cutoff noted by Bowen makes more conflict possible. Given the recent cancellation of a thoughtful program with both agreement and disagreement, it seems our American appetite for conflict is more voracious than ever.

If we were still a part of our original village, having extended family near, we would live being conscious of an outer conscience—in other words, we'd realize that witnesses who've known us all our lives would be aware of our actions. That kind of grounding may become lost in the cutoff that occurred going to the new country.

Some have found ways to recreate this grounding. In the East, and in some rural communities, and for some families in the West as well, there is a great deal of stability. But cutoff affects a large sector of our modern life, and those stable communities may have experienced cutoff from others. This is implied by the observation by political writers that we increasingly live in bubbles or silos of like-minded people.

When we view the increasing incidence of mass shootings and deaths due to police shootings of innocent and unarmed people, it alarms all of us.

Is this further evidence of what Bowen called societal regression? Just as generations of child focus can gradually and eventually produce schizophrenia, generations of conflict and violence can eventually produce senseless wars or the senseless acts of individuals.

A recent shooting occurred at a poolside party in University City, a nice suburb of San Diego. Peter Selis, a middle-aged white male was known to be stressed about his relationship breakup (cutoff), two bankruptcies, and creditors who were hounding him.

All who knew him considered him not at all violent. Yet he sat poolside and shot seven people, coldly killing one while drinking a beer and insisting that his ex-girlfriend stay on the phone with him as he continued shooting. All but one of the victims were people of color, which made it look like a hate crime. Police killed him before he shot more people.

Violence can also turn inward. 2013 Suicide statistics indicate that the tenth leading cause of death for all age ranges is suicide. But for teens, suicide is the second leading cause of death. Is societal regression taking a great toll on our youth?

What are the leading causes of death for teens? Previously, in 2006, accidents and murder were ahead of suicide.

On February 2, 2017, Penn State fraternity brothers ordered nineteen-year-old engineering student and fraternity pledge Timothy Piazza to drink so much alcohol during his hazing ritual that he twice fell down a flight of stairs. He later died from multiple injuries.

Security camera footage revealed that no one assisted him. There was one exception. When one man had the strength to buck the group, and strongly advocated for getting him help, he was knocked into a wall and ordered to leave.

People searching for answers to the deaths, suicides, and murders of our youth might seek a couple of resources that I believe are very valuable. A documentary by filmmaker Jennifer Seibel Newsome is one. She made the 2015 film, *The Mask You Live In*, when pregnant with her first son.

She had great concerns about the way this culture raises boys, and wanted to help make the world a better place for her son and all sons. It helps us to look at the ways in which violence is cultivated in males, while traces of compassion or other culturally-defined feminine qualities are knocked to the wall and ordered out.

That is why the other eighteen frat guys from Penn State were facing charges of aggravated assault with prison sentences of ten to twenty years until the judge dismissed the most serious charges against them in September. However, in November a security camera film that had been deleted was recovered, giving evidence of more brothers being involved in manslaughter, hazing, aggravated assault, and simple assault. One individual was charged with tampering with evidence and obstructing administration of law. Some of the dismissed charges have been reinstated.

NBC News reported an update on December 15, 2017:

A grand jury report blamed Penn State University for allowing a lack of oversight, shoddy record-keeping and an accepted culture of underage drinking and hazing to flourish for years before culminating in the February death of a fraternity pledge.

The long-awaited 236-page report said school administrators "displayed a shocking apathy to the potential danger associated with doing nothing."

Since Piazza's death, at least two other pledges died at other universities in possible hazing episodes according to *the NY Times*.

Piazza's mother, Evelyn, told *NBC News* if the fraternity members had "acted like a brother or a friend or a responsible human being, it would have been a lot different."

We look at such events and use all our defenses to think these are extreme and rare cases. They are not. The grand jury called it an "accepted culture of drinking and hazing…" This is not unique to Penn State. *The Mask You Live In*, a documentary by Jennifer Siebel Newsome, looks deeply into the way our culture deals with boys from a young age.

She created the film while pregnant with her first son to help make the world a better place for him and all boys. Joe Ehrmann, former NFL coach, says in the film that the three most destructive words every boy is told are, "Be a man."

This is a case of control (part of conflict) sliding into violence in the name of fun. Perhaps it is time for thoughtful people to look at the long-term effect of pressuring boys to be supermen, avoiding the qualities that could make them more balanced individuals, capable of practicing understanding, empathy, equality.

The case is still pending as of the publication of this book.

Nonviolent communication

Another important resource for overcoming conflict or violence is *Nonviolent Communication*, by the late Marshall Rosenberg. He grew up in Detroit during the race riots in 1967. As a young Jewish male, the language of violence greeted him daily.

This inspired him to see the roots of violence in our language. We have words that start fights. Chapter 4, Choosing Understanding and Empathy, includes an eye-opening list of words that can easily start fights. They are offered as words that express feelings. But they have a double meaning that confuses and puts the other on the defensive. An example: "I feel ignored," holds a passive accusation that "you ignored me."

The listener may be concerned that the other person didn't have their need for deeper listening met. However, he also feels a need to defend himself against the implied accusation.

Terrorism is another complex form of conflict that draws in youth. It is permeated with violence applied randomly toward groups of people designated as the enemy.

Dr. Daniel Papero, a Bowen specialist, discussed the many factors contributing to societal regression during his 2017 San Diego presentation. He mentioned one factor few are considering, but that he believes is major: the population has grown to eight-and-a-half billion people. Forty-two percent of these are in poverty, and 40 percent are younger than age twenty-five—the majority of whom are male.

He said, "Young, idle males without work are a problem for any society." Terrorist groups work to meet the needs of those youth. Dr. Papero indicated that if we ignore major and complex issues like this, we will never overcome terrorism by attacking it with more war or violence.

Terrorism is extreme conflict directed at strangers. Do you remember my generally principled, loving father's occasional treatment of total strangers on the road? He used a much milder version of the same conflict pattern.

Perhaps we have all been conditioned through cutoff that the standards of behavior we have been taught to practice do not apply to our treatment of strangers. Is that why men who were likely decent at home could offer me verbal assault on the streets? As a stranger, did they see me as having less worth?

Is this how the pattern gets carried into war, where the anonymity somehow gives permission to conquerors to kill and rape innocent people?

Our nation began with a foundation involving cutoff, and we have gradually snowballed into greater violence. The world has reflected a similar course. Cutoff, over time, has dangerous consequence.

On the way to emotional maturity

What did Bowen's observations of emotionally-mature people reveal? How could it help us reverse this increasingly chaotic violence that is permeating our media, our national pastimes (e.g., football), our politics, and our international penchant to solve problems with violence?

We are quite desensitized to violence that occurs at a distance. But when it hits close to home, we can no longer be so detached. Seeing violence up close causes us to grieve the horrific loss or injury our dear friends or loved ones, such as Peter Selis' victims and Timothy Piazza's family and friends now suffer.

Where is the way out of the cycle of conflict for those who are excited by it? It may be wise to first ask, "How did I get here?" Or, less personally, "How did our culture get here?"

ABMs always begin subtly. We slip into them in an emotional moment. Remember how I developed the conflict habit with the men who were cat-calling to me on the street?

ABMs help us feel better temporarily, immediately rewarding our behavior choice. Soon they become habit. Habit grows in intensity until eventually it can become an obsession or addiction. We continually seek more of the drug to give us the same high. For some, their high is a bit of freedom from anxiety. For others, it may be a sense of being a winner or a victor over others.

The benefits of freedom from conflict

My concern now is the national appetite for conflict. Robert Siegel's May 12, 2017 PBS story gives evidence of our craving for, or at least tolerance of conflict.

At the level of conflict our minds and bodies are rippling out, could our society be headed for a major war or other major national negative event?

What would it be like if we, instead, would first free our minds and our relationships from conflict? Could we then tackle the job of significantly reducing the dose we are exposed to from our media and entertainment? I believe this is a useful route to take, beginning at home in our own lives.

. . . .

Beth had learned of the iBE Workshop from her healthcare practitioner who knew about her history of rape, abandonment, and violence in her current home. Beth was very eager to participate.

She completed a history form in which it was clear she had therapist and clergy trauma. I recommended she have three sessions working on those traumas before the workshop. Because I am a therapist, without that work it would be likely she would not trust me. That could interfere with her feeling of safety in the workshop.

Beth was very happy that I recognized her events as traumas, and made the appointments to come in. She decided after two sessions to attend the two-day workshop. Afterward, she wanted two more individual sessions to work on traumas that had been too sensitive to handle in a group setting.

After the workshop, Beth shared:

> She and her fiancé were both disabled by chronic health issues, depression, and PTSD. Thus, they were living with her future in-laws. The in-laws-to-be felt entitled to be extremely demanding of both of them due to their kindness in giving low-cost housing.

> One night the father was demanding something of his son, who didn't jump up quickly enough to do it. Beth was horrified to see father vigorously choke his son from behind. She lost it and attacked the future father-in-law and mother-in-law. This incident was very traumatic for her as she had never behaved like this in her life.

> A few weeks after we processed this memory, Beth shared this: "The iBE workshop experience was indescribable. I feel so much lighter and happier. I'm not reacting to situations the way I did last week. I feel like the old me again, but an even better version."

Later, she gave an update on how things were going with other family members she had been out of contact with. See chapter

6 on connection and patience for that story, because it is based on the new ways she is connecting with people in her life.

Beth also gave an update on improvements in her relationship with her future mother-in-law. Since this deals with the overfunctioning/ underfunctioning pattern, you'll find that story in chapter 10 on balance and equality.

Beth's story taught me that people can overcome significant patterns of conflict and control more efficiently than I could have believed possible. She made a significant turnaround in one month using iBE in group and individual work. As reported at ibetherapy.com/relationshipresources, this is the client whose gross score on the Differentiation of Self Inventory increased by five points by her three-month follow-up.

I believe including EMDR in the process produced the efficiency. She used two individual sessions, a ninety-minute prep night, twelve hours of group and two more individual sessions.

There is reason for hope

Considering the trend of increasing conflict and societal regression, it is easy to feel gloomy. However, there is good reason for optimism. Bowen theory offers direction and hope.

Bowen observed that when one person makes steady efforts at differentiation, others in the system begin to pick up their functioning. Health becomes contagious.

And EMDR offers the AIP to help people transform mental and emotional health rapidly.

In the next chapter, you will learn how to overcome conflict. As more accomplish this in their own lives, the media and our leaders will follow the crowd to maintain an audience.

We each have the potential to become a responsible leader in our own lives. When people step fully into position leading themselves, the magic of Bowen theory manifests. Societal regression can shift to conscientious progression, one person, one home, and one family system at a time.

Wise Confucius expressed it thus:

> If there is righteousness in the heart, there will be beauty in the character.
> If there is beauty in the character, there will be harmony in the home.
> If there is harmony in the home, there will be order in the nations.
> When there is order in the nations, there will peace in the world.

. . . .

At a Glance: Understanding Conflict

- As with all anxiety-binding mechanisms, conflict does not resolve problems. Thus, it increases anxiety and over time becomes a stronger and more intense habit pattern.
- Conflict is often entered automatically, with minimal conscious thought.
- Conflict (including criticism and control messages) often begin with "you." This is the red flag for criticism and judgment.
- Some believe the intensity of conflict shows them they are cared about. Their need to feel important gets confused with conflict.
- Generations of conflict result in domestic violence and/or violence outside the family.
- Conflict causes pain and trauma. According to the ACES study, verbal abuse is the most harmful form of abuse.

- In the conflict style, the focus is on the others' perceived faults instead on one's own part in the problem.

Practical Tips

1. For one month, track your own "you" statements. See how many you make each day and see if simple awareness helps you reduce "you" statements. (Complete steps 2 and 3 to work on this.)
2. When ready, writing down the "you" statements in a column on the left side of a page. In the right column, translate that statement into something more factual and neutral, such as "When I heard you say or saw you do this, I felt this way, because I need _____."
3. Share this information calmly and see if the quality of your conversation with others improves. Continue this effort for one month. Renew the effort any time you find yourself slipping into "you" statements again.

Chapter 4
Choosing Understanding and Empathy

"Wisdom is the principal thing; therefore get wisdom: and with all thy getting get understanding."

Proverbs 4: 7, King James Version (KJV)

"When you see a Crime punished, you may be inwardly Pleased; but always shew Pity to the Suffering Offender."

23rd Rule of Civility, George Washington

"Never criticize a man until you've walked a mile in his moccasins."

Paraphrased from a poem with the original title, Judge Softly, written by Mary T. Lathrap in 1895

Pop Quiz

T or F I have experienced the deep satisfaction of understanding someone in a new way.

T or F I've put my own feelings aside to listen to another person.

T or F Even if feeling upset, I've hung in there with a difficult conversation.

T or F I've overcome conflict with someone and the relationship has improved.

T or F I've experienced that blame and criticism are less satisfying than understanding.

I ask these questions to help you to realize you have sometimes naturally practiced maturity-building principles and emotional maturity. I believe you will become stronger in this practice as you learn from the examples and principles here.

Emotionally-mature responses

Bowen called emotionally-mature people differentiated because they were comfortable being different from others.

The term differentiated comes from biology. When a new cell begins the life of a complex organism such as a human being, the cells are stem cells, full of potential. At some point the first brain cells develop, and the first bone cells. From that time on, they never revert to being another type of cell. They are differentiated.

I generally use the term emotionally-mature, because it is a more familiar term, but you will also see the word differentiated throughout the book.

Responses to conflict

Bowen observed how the most mature people in his life handled conflict. He was curious to know: "How do you handle it when someone is in conflict with you? If someone wants to argue, blame, criticize, or guilt-trip you, how would you respond?"

They described attitudes like this:

> Instead of focusing on conflict, I'd try to hear useful information. I might thank the person for letting me know their opinions and feelings. I'd ask questions so I could sympathize with their concerns as well as possible. I'd listen as calmly as possible, as long as possible. I might respond: 'It helps me understand you better to know how important this is to you. Do you believe I understand you pretty well? Is there anything I'm still not getting?'

> Such approaches tend to soften the other person's distressed feelings. It tends to make him more receptive to listening to my point of view. Most people really

need to be heard and to matter. It calms them. And, it increases the chance that they may become ready to listen to me.

Understanding makes trust, respect, safety, warmth, tenderness, friendship, and love possible. We cannot love a person we don't know, and we won't know a person unless we take time to be curious and understand that person.

In fact, this is the goal I recommend all embrace as they enter a new romance. Build the friendship by taking your time to understand each other thoroughly. This is not as easy as the fun of romance, but it protects the romance for the long term.

Responses to differences

Bowen learned from his own experience and the emotionally-mature people that the more differentiated people knew who they were and were comfortable with themselves. He called their strength, differentiation of self—the ability to be their own unique person. Shakespeare understood this:

> This above all: to thine own self be true,
> And it must follow, as the night the day,
> Thou canst not then be false to any man.

> *(Shakespeare, "Hamlet" act I, scene 3)*

Emotionally-mature people like getting to know and appreciate others as they are. Less emotionally-mature people are sometimes threatened by differences. They may feel insecure if they are not comfortably similar. They may fear judgment, based on past experiences when they were labeled wrong for being different.

When we become more neutral and accepting of differences, we find ourselves more immune to conflict. We can learn to maintain a calm self-acceptance, while being open to understanding others' views.

The same principles apply in any relationship, whether with friends, coworkers, boss, child, or in-law. Take the time to know what makes a person tick. Start with something as basic as asking her what she likes. "And what don't you like? What are your pet peeves?"

This is not always a natural or comfortable process. Some people share easily. Some are more cautious and need time to open up. Take your time and savor the process.

There are ways to make the process a game. Invite one another to go shopping and look at any kind of object: art, technical, fashion, taste treats. Discover what each other prefers.

Online surveys can be interesting to complete, sharing the results with each other. I particularly like Dr. Martin Seligman's website, authentichappiness.org. Under the Questionnaires tab you can browse a number of surveys about your character strengths, optimism, gratitude, or grit. I love his VIA Survey of Character Strengths that comes in both standard version and children's versions. It is necessary to register and login to access his surveys. However, you can opt to not receive any emails from them.

Another brilliant yet simple concept is from Gary Chapman, author of *The 5 Love Languages®: The Secret to Love that Lasts*. His website, 5lovelanguages.com, offers a quick survey to help you identify your love language. People often have challenges in relationships because they assume or expect others to value and offer the same love language they need. For example, one partner might prefer affectionate touch, gift giving, quality time, words of affirmation, or acts of service.

Often couples do not speak or hear the same love language. It can leave one or both of them feeling mightily unloved until they understand this difference between them. For example, your loved one may be doing all she can to affirm you, thinking you need this. But maybe you need acts of service that show her love.

Thus, I recommend reading chapter 9 in Chapman's book, "Discovering Your Primary Love Language." Discuss it together to understand your language, and your partner's language. Then I suggest reading the chapter on your partner's love language. It can help you if that language feels foreign. Wouldn't it be nice to move beyond the boundaries of your own habits and closer to the heart of your own unique dear one?

Relationship building

To build a close relationship, we sometimes feel vulnerable venturing into the unknown with another person. One risk is that we learn we are wrong about the person. Another is that we may change our view because we now see deeper and broader.

We may get past a grudge or a prejudice. Sometimes we have a prejudice toward someone in our own family, for example, our youngest sibling. We see them as a kid when they are twenty-five-, thirty-five-, or forty-five-years-old. We haven't updated our view while our sibling has been constantly updating, learning from experience, blooming, and achieving more of his or her potential.

I had this experience. I love all my siblings but had a special bond with my youngest sister. She was born when I was eleven and had a giant desire for a baby of my own. I am very grateful my parents provided one!

When she was seven, I headed off to college. In my *naiveté*, I didn't realize the need to keep in touch with her weekly. I called my parents but not her or my other siblings. There was no good reason for this omission. My parents didn't think to correct me.

The end result? By the time I graduated, we had become near strangers. It took effort and persistence to overcome that sad, strange, disconnected feeling.

Understanding requires listening and a sincere curiosity about the other's perceptions, feelings, values, needs, and experience. With time and practice, the process of understanding deepens as the relationship continues with stability, life, and fun.

When a person has an intent to argue or push their own view onto you until they score a win, it can disarm him if you express curiosity about his point of view and his feelings. If you intend to really understand, you will often see the speaker take a big breath.

That's always a good sign. Your companion is relaxing and feeling safer. We humans each have a very deep need to be heard, seen, and understood.

Dealing with a critical spouse

Alice and Geoff, a less mature couple, are having an emotional ping-pong match.

> Alice: Geoff, you're making those clicking noises with your mouth again.
>
> Geoff: What's it to you? You are way too controlling!
>
> Alice: I'm just asking you to be polite. If you don't care about me, can't you care about setting a good example for the kids?
>
> Geoff: So, you are accusing me of not being polite now?

This argument is just beginning. It is full of blame, accusation, judgment, and assumptions. Note one similarity in the messages: they are "you" statements. "You" statements are perceived as fighting words. The assumption is that the speaker knows more about you than you do.

This is perfect fuel for argument for anyone who wants to get one going. I'm not saying conflict is guaranteed. It takes two to fight—just like it takes two hands hitting one another to applaud.

Let's see now how a more mature Geoff and Alice could respond to Alice's critical comment.

> Alice: Geoff, I'm hearing those clicking noises with your mouth again.
>
> Geoff: Hmm, I wasn't even aware of it. Thanks for bringing it to my attention.
>
> Alice: You know I don't like it. Why do you continue to do it? (She slips into conflict mode, after a good clean start.)
>
> Geoff (Remaining thoughtful, he takes a breath and begins thinking of the conflict challenges his parents dealt with. He remembers Alice, too, grew up with discounting messages and begins to feel more compassion for her. He smiles at Alice with his eyes): Are you thinking that my habit affects my love for you?
>
> Alice catches the softness in his eyes: No, I can see it doesn't.
>
> Geoff: I love you enough to work on this stupid habit of mine. If I click unconsciously, will you remind me by just saying, 'click?'
>
> Alice: Sure, honey! I really appreciate your willingness!

How to understand one another

Take your time to gain a bigger, more complete view of the other person. Try to really see things from his or her perspective as you walk in the other person's moccasins.

Ask simple questions that start with "What, When, Where, How"—anything but "Why?" Why questions automatically put people on the defense. Best to avoid them. One "What" question would be: "What experiences helped you to see this?"

As you ask one or two thoughtful questions (beware of probing beyond comfort), you offer a gift of increasing calmness. This peace allows your friend or loved one to open up more brain and heart territory.

Calm reasoning and calm feeling become feasible, and then possible. You will be receiving an added bonus: by growing in understanding, you can have rich conversations and connection throughout life.

It eventually becomes clear that conflict is generally due to misunderstanding, whether of self, of other, or both.

What if my feelings are hurt?

This all sounds very nice, but, you may ask: How about when the conflictual person really hurt your feelings? The words still echo in the cavern of your mind. They haven't lost their charge. What if you don't have the inner generosity to listen at all? I see several options here.

1. Since I know the value and efficiency of EMDR, I suggest a session or two for the individual feeling hurt, to desensitize the words of judgment and feelings of rejection. As we process the anger, hurt, or sadness and grief about the cruel words, clients often spontaneously express compassion for the individual hurting them (they rarely feel compassion until the negativity is neutralized).

2. Use the Bowen approach to assume the calm curiosity of a researcher, delving deeper into the mindset of the research subject (who in this case could be a loved one, friend, coworker, or neighbor).

3. If the conflict is domestic violence, call the police or a domestic violence hotline. Once you are safe, please seek help from a therapist specializing in the treatment of domestic violence.

4. If the person behaves cruelly or without civility, yet you must work with him at work or contend with her as an ex-spouse, boundaries are an essential resource.

    a. You might use "I" statements (explained in chapter 11) such as, "I don't listen to name-calling or put-downs." Or, "I don't accept controlling language. I will listen to respectful description of what is a problem for you. Let me know when you are ready to try again."

    b. Make notes of such behavior if it is a workplace occurrence. It may help if you seek a manager's guidance. Working with such a person is becoming more common. As of 2017, 29 percent of Americans believe this country has a major civility problem.

    c. Make sure to access your support system to keep you in close connection with the most trusted and respectful people in your life.

5. You could use an approach recommended by all religions: forgiveness.

    a. An excellent resource for this is *Forgive for Good: A Proven Prescription for Health and Happiness*, by Dr. Fred Luskin.

    b. Forgiveness is easier when you can leave a person behind. If the person is toxic, it may be wise to make this a high priority. If it's not possible, see the section "Wise triangling may be useful" in chapter 8.

6. You could use empathy and compassion.

a. Marshall B. Rosenberg, PhD, wrote an excellent book for cultivating empathy: *Nonviolent Communication: A Language of Life.*

Rosenberg (1999, 2003, 2015) practiced the method described in his book during hundreds of opportunities to mediate between individuals, gangs or tribes in conflict or war. In his own words:

> About eight years ago, I was mediating between a Muslim tribe and a Christian tribe in northern Nigeria. In their conflict, a quarter of the population had been killed. At that time, they were fighting about how many places in the marketplace each side would have to display their products. I started the reconciliation process with them by saying that I was confident that if we could hear each other's needs, we could find a way to get everyone's needs met. Inviting whoever wanted to start, I asked: 'What needs of yours are not getting met?' The chief from the Christian tribe screamed, 'You people are murderers!' Notice that when I asked him what needs weren't getting met, his response was to tell me what was wrong with the other side. This provoked a counter judgment. Somebody on the Muslim side screamed back, 'You've been trying to dominate us! We're not going to tolerate it anymore!'

> Because our training is based on the assumption that all violent language is a tragic expression of unmet needs, when the chiefs finished screaming, my job was to translate the enemy image of 'murderer' into language describing the needs of the person who screamed. I said, 'Chief, are you saying that your need for safety is not being met and you want some agreement that no matter what the conflict, that it will be resolved some way other than violence?' He looked shocked for a

moment because this is different from how people are trained to think. Then he said, 'That's exactly right!'

But getting the chief to acknowledge his need wasn't enough. I had to get the Muslim side to see through their enemy image. I said, 'Would somebody on the other side, please tell me what you heard the chief say his needs were?'

A gentleman from the Muslim tribe screamed back, 'Then why did you kill my son?' In fact, there were several others in the Muslim tribe who knew that someone present had killed one of their children. So there were a lot of feelings. The Muslim tribe had to put down their rage long enough to hear the needs of the Christian tribe. And that wasn't easy. I had to give them some empathy before they could do that. But finally, I got them to hear just one simple thing, that the Christian tribe had said they had a need for safety.

It took me about an hour and a half to get both sides to release the enemy image long enough to hear a need of the other side. At that point one of the chiefs came up and said to me, 'If we know how to communicate this way, we don't have to kill each other!' (Kabatznick and Cullen, 2004)

Rosenberg became a genius of empathy. If you want to gain more skill in empathy, please read his book for further growth. Enthusiasts of nonviolent communication (NVC), offer practice groups at a nominal fee in many cities around the country. For people who haven't experienced empathy in their lives, this is a rich resource for growth.

Empathy is what helps you to walk a mile in someone else's moccasins (Lathrap, 1895). As you put yourself into another's life, you can finally see though his eyes or hear through her ears, as the Muslims began to do for the Christians in the example above. Or as I learned to do with my mother.

I found Mom was holding herself back from loving because she loved so much. Unresolved trauma can have that effect. Their actions may appear crazy, but it is only because we do not understand. As an EMDR therapist, I find that when we take the healing journey with any person, all their habits, foibles, and symptoms eventually become clear. As they become clear with self-empathy, healing is very close.

Limited license to disagree and criticize

Bowen was not opposed to having some conflict. For families that specialize in a peace/agree style, he deliberately encouraged making room for disagreement.

I believe it is a wise step for all couples, and even for siblings to have such discussions. Parents are wise to supervise and guide initially, and thereafter, occasionally catch their children using empathy, understanding, curious interest and active listening. Always realize that what you pay attention to will grow. Please pay the most attention to positive behavior and strengths.

In chapter 3 I promised to let you know more about what helped me overcome my anger and criticism habit. My husband and I benefitted from wise guidance.

Our minister advised us about how to resolve and reduce conflict. He said, "Schedule a once a week meeting in which all criticisms, disagreements, or disappointments are saved to share."

During the week, if someone blurted out a criticism (such as myself), my husband would say, "Save it for the criticism meeting Monday night." I'd agree, and then go make a note of it. That is an essential step. It is easy to forget things that seem urgently important when the emotion is triggered.

The nice thing about arriving at our 7 to 7:30 p.m. meeting was that we were both calm and prepared to receive complaints. By then, the primitive blame instinct was toned down. We were saved from the need to defend ourselves. We saved time and emotional energy.

Sometimes we reached agreement. Usually we reached more understanding that there was a positive motive behind the criticism. We were generally interested in the welfare of one another or of the whole family, and that was comforting.

Other times we agreed to disagree, because we had a value difference or a basic personality difference. These cases are perpetual problems, according to marriage researchers John and Julie Gottman. They are differences that will exist for the lifetime of the relationship. Every relationship has some of these.

My husband and I worked to achieve a very good, happy marriage. But we, too, had perpetual problems. We learned to accept the irreconcilable differences.

In mature relationships, perpetual problems can still be discussed. They are not treated with tension or silence. If they are, the danger is that they become gridlocked, perpetual problems that cause resentment about the fact that the other person will never change in the desired direction. The desire gets surrendered by acknowledging it, yielding peace and harmony in the relationship.

Of course, sometimes an irreconcilable difference is so major that it is not possible to continue the relationship. That is a very personal decision left to the individual.

The great value of criticism meetings is that they allow a somewhat calmer flow of information, promoting understanding. Sometimes the greatest wisdom is simply, "I accept you as you are, even if we have a major difference. Wouldn't life be dull if we were identical in every way?"

I generally recommend these meetings be between two people rather than an entire family. Family meetings are useful for different purposes, such as planning, taking a position that may have been inspired at one of the one-to-one meetings, problem-solving, and so on.

These meetings can be called for even after children launch and leave home. If a difference arises that causes emotion, any family member can propose to meet to increase understanding.

Chief Joe Medicine Crow—courage and compassion

World War II American Hero, Joe Medicine Crow, courageously brought wisdom and understanding into the practice of war, and in the process became a Crow War Chief. The Chief demonstrated the possibility of practicing conflict without bringing it inside one's heart, mind, or soul.

We might have a lot less PTSD from war if we trained our soldiers like the Crow train their chiefs. Our way often brings the conflict inside where it can fester for years or decades in the form of that terrible disorder (PTSD) that makes people feel limited, stuck, or even crazy. They feel ashamed and thus don't want to share with people who want to understand them.

If you know of such a person, please let them know about EMDR therapy. Veterans have demonstrated a preference for EMDR, because they don't have to share details about what happened. They only have to be willing to think and feel about it for thirty seconds at a time. Soon they discover the horrible feelings are fading.

Let's return to Chief Joe. Joe Medicine Crow (2016) entered World War II with the goal of becoming a Crow War Chief. Four clear tasks are required to earn this position:

1. **Touch an enemy without killing him**
   Joe came across a German soldier while scouting through woods. He won a battle of hand-to-hand combat but didn't kill the German.

2. **Take an enemy's weapon**
   Joe took the enemy's weapon during the above incident.

3. **Lead a successful war party**
   Joe led seven soldiers to get dynamite from a lost allied position. He completed the mission without losing a single man.

4. **Steal an enemy's horse**
   Nazi soldiers took a thoroughbred farm. Joe sneaked past sleeping guards and found the best horse. Using a rope as his bridle, he mounted the horse bareback with a Crow war cry. He herded fifty horses out of the corral and into the night.

When a human accomplishes steps that fit the highest ideals of courage and compassion, as did Chief Joe Medicine Crow, he earns the respect not only of his people but himself. And he earns the respect of the wider world. On June 25, 2008 at a ceremony in Montana, Chief Joe received the Bronze Star from the U.S. Army, and the French Legion of Honor Chevalier medal, both for service during World War II. He was awarded the Congressional Medal of Honor in 2009 by President Obama.

Can we work toward a medal of honor of our own? What standards would inspire, motivate, and fuel our efforts?

From getting to understanding

I have worked in my lifetime to shift a bit from a getting mindset to an understanding mindset. This doesn't mean that getting, accumulating, or having nice things is wrong. It's a question of balance. If we neglect understanding, people in our lives will be suffering. If we practice understanding, what benefits and blessings might come from that?

I can only speak for myself and my family, including my extended family and friends. We value time to be together, to talk, to exchange ideas and feelings. Such connection feeds my soul.

Even consumer purchases can be an opportunity to gain understanding of each other and our desires. For me, having humble belongings frees me from the pressure to be a super woman or a super mom. I never really liked either title because of the pressure for perfection (as judged by others) that is implied. Also, I don't want to work that hard!

I am content to be an understanding person who lives in simple comfort and beauty. Perhaps I'll give myself a medal of honor for that. No ceremony. Just gratitude and contentment. I am grateful to have had a husband who made understanding a high priority in our marriage. He said that when you are married to a therapist you have no choice! But I know he had a choice and I am grateful for the ones he made.

I am grateful to have a son who has learned the importance of understanding and the other maturity-building principles such as connection, direct personal committed relationships, and living a balanced life, respectful of all. He is thus appreciated by many. His in-laws say he is amazing. To me this is wealth beyond things—a wealth gained from the practice of understanding.

The Bible verse is insightful. May we all be blessed with just a little more understanding, and reap the harvest.

Distance is the next anxiety-binding mechanism we will address. It is a challenge that can delay but not prevent understanding.

. . . .

At a Glance: Choosing Understanding and Empathy

- Giving understanding can calm the other person. Then you can invite that person to try to understand your point of view.
- Invite others to get curious about how you are different and ways you are similar.
- Understanding oneself is very important in life. Each day ask yourself, "How can I be true to myself today?"
- Go on a journey of discovery to appreciate differences in yourself and others. Useful tools: VIA Character Strengths Survey and *5 Love Languages*.
- It can be hard to understand another if the person hurt your feelings. Work to understand yourself first, if possible, or seek a friend who can give you understanding and empathy. When you feel ready, invite the other to talk and share how their actions affected you.
- When people realize you want to understand them, they feel relief and hope.

Practical Tips

1. To gain understanding, listen curiously and calmly, as long as possible. Strive to put yourself in the other person's shoes to understand how they think, feel, and behave. Try to identify the feelings they may be having. You don't have to be right. If you try, the other person will correct you if you are wrong. That supports the goal of understanding.
2. If you aren't able to listen calmly at first, express that you want to do so once you feel more calm.

3. Study people who have gained understanding. For instance, you could read the autobiographies or memoirs of Nelson Mandela (1994), Chief Joe Medicine Crow (2006) or others. *Nonviolent Communication* (Rosenberg) could be called a bible of understanding.

Chapter 5
Understanding Distance

"Father, forgive them, for they know not what they do."

Luke 23:34 KJV

"Love your neighbor as yourself."

Mark 12:31; Leviticus 19:18

Said emphatically to his fellow countrymen: "There is no future without forgiveness."

Archbishop Desmond Tutu, chair of South Africa's Truth and Reconciliation Commission

Pop Quiz

T or F I live in a bubble that keeps me separate from people with differing views.

T or F When I am uncomfortable with someone's behavior or speech, I withdraw.

T or F Distance and avoidance are my safe places.

T or F I have broken off relationships suddenly without allowing any discussion.

T or F I've experienced pain when someone has cut off from me. It still bothers me.

Distance or cutoff

Distance in our relationships can be emotional distance, such as ignoring a message, changing the subject, or other discounting actions or comments that weaken relationships. It can also be geographic distance.

Sometimes people deal with a difficult relationship by moving to another state. But it is possible to have emotional distance when living in the same town as other relatives. And it is achievable to maintain emotional connection despite many miles of geographic separation.

When describing extreme distance and lack of emotional contact, Murray Bowen used the term cutoff.

To some extent, immigrants coming to America in previous centuries were risking or even choosing a cutoff from family back home. We are all either immigrants or natives who have been removed from our native lands in one way or another. If we are practicing distance, we have a lot of company.

Either we or our forbearers had many motivations for leaving the home country. The reason was often survival. Some historical sources say that even indigenous peoples left the Asian peninsula 12,000 years ago before migrating to this continent.

We or our ancestors often escaped something, whether it be drought, poverty, cruelty, or oppression—either small-scale (in the family) or large-scale war.

We may have dropped out of communication simply due to the sheer difficulty of it. Or perhaps our clear intention was to break all ties to the dangers or grudges left behind. Either way, we began a pattern, and that pattern has consequences.

Immigrants

As we can witness in Syria and Mexico today, when people migrate, they generally do so under stressed conditions.

My Norwegian great grandfathers on both sides came to the US in the late 1800s because of poverty. They were not the oldest sons. Only the oldest sons had a chance in Norway, because they were the inheritors of the family farm. So my forefathers each traveled alone to a new country.

Eventually, after a series of more cutoffs, they both reached small rural communities in North Dakota, just two to ten miles from each other's families.

When they left their country, they had to distance themselves from everything they had known to that point in their lives:

- Loved ones, mothers and fathers, brothers, and sisters
- The home they grew up in
- The community they grew up in
- Their Lutheran church pastor and community of like-minded souls
- Their language
- Their culture and musical instruments
- Their books
- Their government and customs
- Their food
- Their style of dress, footwear, etc.

Where did your forerunners (foreigners) emigrate from? Did they come due to poverty, like mine did?

Africans came against their will on slave ships where many died on the way due to deplorable conditions.

The Irish came due to the potato famine.

Mexicans have been coming due to the poverty and/or out-of-control violence during the last fifty years.

Jews who could escape the march of Nazi Germany across Europe arrived in America and elsewhere, usually due to a series of miracles and heroic efforts of others to hide, shelter, and protect them.

Vietnamese came due to the devastation of war in their beautiful country.

Iraqi residents who are Chaldean Christians (devout Catholics) were persecuted in Iraq. Many had witnessed their loved ones slaughtered and fled with their families for their lives.

Somalis endured genocide. Hidden children were left standing after their villages were slaughtered by machine-gun toting soldiers. Many of them became the lost children of Somalia who helped one another survive, and eventually come to America.

All these immigrants endured trauma of one form or another. A percentage of them, in the context of cutoff (which could imply a severely reduced support system), could likely be diagnosed with post-traumatic stress disorder (PTSD).

Knowing the hardships faced by these brave ancestors or more recent relatives can help to temper, a bit, our view of ancestors with tempers.

Most of them immigrated at a time when a mailed letter took months to reach the recipient. For slaves and the most devastated immigrants, there was a total cutoff in communication to all who were left behind. They lost a lot of what supported their strength.

For others, the cutoff was not total, but massive. Letters were their lifeblood to keep in touch, to cultivate the most precious of those relationships left behind. Why the most precious? Because once they arrived in the new country, they had a colossal adjustment ahead of them.

The first step was to receive a new name at Ellis Island. My grandfather was told, "I'm sick of 'Larsons,' can't you think of something else?" On the spot my great-grandfather had to choose a new name. He thought of the beautiful Ølken lake near his farm. "How about Ølken?" The American agent didn't know how to hear or write Ø, so he said, "OK, Elken it is!"

The history of distance we Americans share has set us up for some vulnerability. Because the distance often continues for generations, we get comfortable with it. It can become a habit—a habit that limits our connections and our support system.

Natives

In San Diego, when I arrived in 1986, many bumper stickers proudly proclaimed, "San Diego Native since 1950" or some other decade. People were not happy to have new people moving in, because the overwhelming influx had totally changed the geography and the lifestyle. This was a smaller version of the nationalistic distrust of outsiders that has been displayed by some Americans recently. Whether we trust or distrust, it is wise to ask questions of ourselves. Where did I learn my attitude? Is it reality-based?

I often asked: were these self-proclaimed natives really natives? Or are your people the true natives? Were your forerunners not foreigners, but indigenous people living here for generations, and centuries in relationship with Mother Earth? What was it like for them when newcomers immigrated to America?

Adjustment to cutoff applies to immigrants and natives alike. My grandfather had to get a new name. Eventually many natives were also forced to get "good Christian names."

Adjusting to change is an ongoing human necessity. We may adjust by increasing our distance, or by being open to new experience and new understandings. What is your style for approaching change and new people?

After getting a new name, what came next?

Immigrants are suddenly faced with numerous challenges to adjust to their new land. They needed to:

- Learn the new language of English
- Be socially or legally pressured to give up their old language (my Norwegian family wanted to become Americans and did not teach their children Norwegian)
- Learn new customs
- Learn the words that are not literal, but idioms (very confusing)
- Figure out new geography and climate
- Find a friend or two
- Find a religious connection and work hard to maintain religious roots
- Find a kind mentor or teacher to help interpret all confusing things (if lucky)
- Find a safe place to live, often shared with other poverty-stricken immigrants or natives who speak your language (if lucky)

Lots of stress, trauma, and death can befall vulnerable people making so many adjustments. In their own trauma, some inflict trauma on others.

Distance affects us in many more ways

Beyond the major cutoff of immigration, does distance touch us in our daily lives?

Many more subtle forms of distance can arouse sensitivity and cause increasing problems in our relationships. Common distance challenges you may have experienced:

- Ignoring a comment or a subject important to you
- Changing the subject without acknowledgement
- Walking out of the room suddenly, without a word
- Storming out of the room to avoid an argument

- Tiptoeing around someone, and even hiding, to avoid all arguments
- Looking down at a cell phone rather than up at the nearby people
- Experiencing a breakup or divorce, either quickly, or with a long, slow, contentious process
- Coping with the death of a loved one, a natural, inevitable form of distance
- Being disowned as a punishment
- Becoming depressed—associated with distance, as people avoid contact with others
- Committing suicide—the ultimate form of a chosen cutoff, with no return
- Dying—a cutoff without a choice

The phenomenon of breaking up

Most of us have never been trained in certain basic life skills. Breaking up is one of those—it's an important, though sad skill, because it happens in our lives regardless of how much we might prefer it didn't.

If you were taught how to break up in a positive way, you are lucky indeed. If so, please let me know how you were taught, because I would be fascinated.

As a therapist, I know many breakups become traumatic to the point they cause PTSD. Research published in 2005 by Mol et al. reported that indeed, a bad breakup can cause the symptoms of PTSD.

This is despite the current American Psychiatric Association standard stating that one must have experienced or witnessed a life-threatening event to have PTSD. PTSD is the only diagnosis that technically requires experiencing a specific kind of event. It assumes that a physical, life-threatening attack is the worst. But research by Felitti (1998) has demonstrated that the most damaging form of childhood abuse is emotional or verbal abuse. The current standard for a PTSD diagnosis omits that finding.

Humans are social creatures, not turtles. Few of us will ever do well totally alone. When one of our most significantly-supportive and bonded relationships ends painfully, we go through the common stages of grief often mixed with panic, and a shaken trust in others that may extend to all men, or all women.

Several factors affect how painful or devastating the loss is:

- The depth of your relationship, closeness, togetherness
- Your level of emotional maturity
- The facts about this unique breakup or loss
- The collection of additional stressors that predated and surrounded the separation
- Your history, and family history around breakups or deaths
- The age of any children who are impacted
- Your current stage in life

Breakups are always painful

They can be done with maturity (consideration for both sides) or selfish immaturity. It makes a major difference in the degree of pain involved. There is not space in this book to give this the full attention it deserves. My second book on emotional maturity will go deeper into this topic, with vivid stories of traumatic breakups and one gentle breakup.

Forgiveness

It is said that the continuation of the species depends on man being forgiving—but it's easier said than done. Few of us have much training in forgiveness.

My mother-in-law, Beverly, gave me lovely training when I was dating my husband. He was a starving student with an old car. When he lent it to me, he forgot to tell me that the gas gauge didn't work. I drove thirty miles and ran out of gas in a parking lot across the street from a car wash. I asked if they might have gas on hand. The employee said, "Yes! You can use this gas can." But when I started the car, it coughed and died. Apparently, there had been detergent in the gas can. The car was destroyed.

David's parents came to pick me and the car up and take me back to San Diego. As we discussed it, I said that maybe we should sue the car wash. Beverly said, "Oh, we wouldn't do that. They were trying to help you. We don't believe in lawsuits."

I took a big breath of fresh air. This is what understanding looks like, rather than blame and criticism.

If you have little experience with forgiveness, either by witnessing it or practicing it yourself, an excellent guide is Fred Luskin's, *Forgive for Good*. The book provides a nine-step, research-proven process.

Death, the distance we can't avoid

Bowen had a unique awareness of death and grieving. His father was an undertaker in a small Tennessee town. Bowen's constant exposure to life and death, and his father's wise and caring example, helped him pay attention to grief as he studied families.

Bowen learned through his research that if people don't openly grieve the loss of a loved one, there will be more symptoms in the family within eighteen months. These symptoms could be physical, emotional, or social (such as isolation, drinking, or law-breaking behavior).

There are mature and healthy ways to approach the deaths of loved ones, friends, and even ourselves. This will be addressed in my future follow-up book.

I spent a couple of years serving as a hospice social worker and counselor for the dying and their family members, and for surviving family members. I witnessed and felt compassion for their challenges and pain. My purpose was to help them get through their situations in the healthiest ways by balancing the needs of self and others.

Yes, I hoped to help the dying have peace and a measure of emotional well-being in the midst of physical difficulty. But with my Bowen perspective, I also encouraged the dying to consider how they might strengthen family relationships for the long-term.

For those who were afraid of their impending death, I suggested reading Raymond Moody's *Life After Life* and to watch the excellent video by the same name. The video features interviews and dramatizations of six people about their own near-death experience (NDE).

Although these people had different religious backgrounds (including one who was an atheist who described himself as a dialectical materialist and scientist) the book and movie described that they all had beautiful, uplifting experiences. The atheist changed his own beliefs significantly based on his own NDE.

They learned that they could not die. They became aware that their own individuality and life continued beyond the loss of the physical body. One said that death is not an end, but just a door to go through. None of them had any fear of going through that door in the future when it became the right time to depart this world.

It is not easy to face one's own death calmly, realistically, living each day to the fullest, and keeping up the commitments in his or her relationships. But it is possible, and it strengthens each relationship and each person connected to the person facing serious illness.

My dear husband David, when faced with cancer, did it with a lot of love, faith, and joy. He was so remarkable and courageous that he will be the subject of one of my next books.

We all face a kind of distance we don't have much choice about: the deaths of our loved ones, our friends, and ourselves. Bowen considered this a very important topic. There are more mature and healthy ways to approach it. This will be addressed in the future follow-up book.

Funerals or memorial services

During my hospice career and since, I met people who had the attitude that they want to spare their loved ones the pain of a funeral or memorial service. It is a nice thought, if that could help. Sadly, I don't believe it does.

Funerals and memorial services are primarily for the living. They provide an opportunity for people who loved or cared about the departed to savor the memories, to share feelings and the tears of grief, to connect with one another, and to strengthen their own bonds and relationships.

Death reminds us that all relationships will end in separation in one way or another. We need to savor each relationship we care about. Funerals or memorial services become true family reunions. They help families rather than hurt them. Yes, loss is painful. That can't be avoided. Avoiding funerals won't solve the pain of loss.

People who think funerals are hurtful often had childhood trauma connected with a funeral of their parent or grandparent. One of my hospice clients was forced to kiss the cold hand of her grandmother in the coffin. Thus, she didn't want a funeral. She thought it would cause great pain for her grandchildren. But she reconsidered her position.

When she died, her young granddaughter was present. She walked up and lovingly held her grandmother's hand spontaneously.

I can say from experience that facing overwhelming pain and loss is softened by the sympathy of each loved one who reaches out.

When there is no service for an important person in my life, I personally feel shaken. My need to honor, savor, and celebrate that life is not going to be easily met. I have actually felt cheated!

On occasion, my need was so great that I organized an informal service to allow a healing experience for those who wanted it. Personally, I found it valuable. The others who participated affirmed how much it meant to them.

I understand that when a loved one declares their insistence on having no service, it sets up conflicting loyalties. Are you to be loyal to your loved one, or loyal to your own heart and its need to not grieve alone?

If you can, discuss this with your loved one before they pass. Let them know that there is no way they can spare you the pain of their departure, though you appreciate their attempt. Yes, funerals and memorial services are sad, but there is also the joy of connection, the heart-touching experiences of sympathy and caring, and the building or rebuilding of relationships. You might share this chapter with your loved one to get the conversation moving.

If you didn't discuss it ahead of time, you can discuss it afterward. According to the near-death experience literature, those who have gone on are not in a distant world, but in a subtler world that co-exists with ours. They can feel our thoughts and feelings much more clearly than we can perceive theirs. So, express the truth of your heart to your loved one and see how it feels. I believe you may receive an assurance that your wishes are just fine.

Within days of the time my husband left his body, I knew I would go to a strengthening convocation of our church in Los Angeles. It's similar to an educational retreat. It was not easy to go to a place with thousands of people and many of my friends. I knew I would feel rather exposed in my pain and loss. So, I spread the word among my local friends that I would love to receive silent hugs, but to not talk.

They let me know how grateful they were that I spelled out my need, because they dearly wanted to know how to help. I can tell you that the sweet sympathy in their eyes healed me so much! It worked out better than I could have dreamed.

We held our memorial service for David almost a month after his passing. It was very satisfying to help create the service and invite others who also wanted and needed to honor him. Bowen taught me to make room for the agendas of others. That allowed others to be creative and make lovely and meaningful contributions.

It is helping my grief to dedicate this book, in part, to David. And, since he called this book "our book," I know his joy is growing as our book nears publication. He believed in it and in my mission to bring greater peace to humankind.

Each thing I dedicate to David helps me feel connected to his great peace and love. It is terribly sad to confront his physical absence from my life now that I'm past the initial shock. Daily I shed tears. I try to balance them with tears of gratitude for all he gave of himself and continues to give.

He is showing me, in truth, that love is the greatest connector. It has the power to overcome distance.

. . . .

At a Glance: Understanding Distance and Cutoff

- When distance becomes a habit, it limits our connections and our support system.
- Whether we ignore someone's concern, change the subject, or walk away, it causes pain or anxiety.
- Adjusting to change is an ongoing human necessity. We may adjust by increasing our distance, or by being open to new experience and new understandings.
- Depression is associated with distance, as people withdraw from others and their support system appears to dwindle.
- Emotionally-mature people end relationships (if necessary) honestly, responsibly, and kindly. This minimizes the pain of the break-up. Poorly done breakups can cause trauma and depression, resulting in trust problems. When traumatic, EMDR may be a useful resource for overcoming these issues efficiently.
- Death is a separation that will happen in our lives. Grieving openly with others is recommended. Bowen found that when this doesn't happen, symptoms (physical, emotional, or social, such as addictions or law-breaking behavior) arise in the family system within eighteen months.
- Forgiveness helps us to overcome an intense urge to distance ourselves due to commitment to a grudge. If the person is unsafe, it is possible to forgive yet maintain a safe physical distance.
- If the person is basically safe, it is helpful if you are able to at least connect neutrally. Sometimes the relationship can be fully repaired and become better than ever.

Practical Tips

1. If depressed, make a list of the people with whom you have been able to share real things. Every other day, reach out to one or more of them and rebuild the connection. Then see what level of depression you feel.

2. Is there someone you are distant from that you miss? A first step is to imagine overcoming the break in your relationship. Remember what is positive about the person and your relationship.

Chapter 6
Choosing Connection and Patience

"A relationship is like a house. When a lightbulb burns out you do not go and buy a new house, you fix the light bulb."

Unknown

"Patience is not sitting and waiting, it is foreseeing. It is looking at the thorn and seeing the rose, looking at the night and seeing the day. Lovers are patient and know that the moon needs time to become full."

Rumi

"If we could look into each other's hearts and understand the unique challenges each of us faces, I think we would treat each other much more gently, with more love, patience, tolerance, and care."

Marvin J. Ashton

"One cannot forgive too much. The weak can never forgive. Forgiveness is the attribute of the strong."

Mahatma Gandhi, 1931

Pop Quiz

T or F I have reconnected with and forgiven someone whom I wrote off for a time.

T or F When I cut off from someone, they don't exist anymore.

T or F When I move to a new location, I maintain close relationships despite the miles.

T or F I find it hard to share what is really going on with me emotionally.

T or F When someone cuts off abruptly from me, I work patiently to repair our connection.

Emotionally-mature relationships

Bowen learned from the differentiated, emotionally-mature people that when others distanced from them, they patiently worked toward connection. They highly valued connection—real, heart-felt, emotional connection.

This did not mean dutiful, bland visits to relatives, friends, or coworkers in which weather, sports, politics, or the latest celebrity gossip were the only topics of conversation. These people were fully present, truly interested in others as well as themselves as whole beings.

Repair skills

Bowen wondered how emotionally-mature people would handle distance if someone were trying to avoid them. What he learned expressed these attitudes:

> I'd connect. I'd reach out to the person letting them know that I miss them and wonder if anything is wrong. I'd invite them to get together sometime soon to try to understand each other better and rectify any wrong.

> And if they didn't respond or made excuses to not get together, I'd try more ways to reach them, patiently, creatively, and perhaps monthly or annually until we finally connected and had a chance to understand each other. I wouldn't give up, but I wouldn't be pushy, either.

Such efforts represent repair skills. Gandhi's quote at the beginning of this chapter mentioned one essential repair skill: forgiveness. This will be given more attention in chapter 8.

A new meaning for well-connected

Bowen learned differentiated people were emotionally well-connected with almost everyone in their extended family system, in their work place, in their neighborhood, and in any organization to which they belonged. Their connection habits gave them a fantastic support system, inoculating them somewhat against stress. If they faced a challenge, they had many to turn to.

I have put this into practice personally, inspired by the differentiated people. It has been very helpful. I do reach out for emotional support, creative ideas, or solutions, for prayer, and even practical help of a physical nature if necessary (such as when there is illness in the family and as caregiver, I'm overwhelmed.)

Having a trusted support system is a wonderful way to strengthen yourself throughout life. These people become your teachers and examples. Yet they are more than that. They are friends with whom you can relax and play. Also, by being in others' support systems, you know that you are contributing to helping them live happier and better lives, too.

Such connection was not my natural mode. When I began my Bowen study, I was naturally a very shy person, an introvert. I was a good listener, but not so good at sharing about my own realities, my thoughts, and feelings. For one thing, I assumed no one would be interested. I had to work up a pretty good sense of upset in order to share personally.

Looking back to my initial introduction to Bowen theory, if I were asked to count the people with whom I could share and listen mutually and equally concerning ourselves and our lives, I could probably think of three people: my father, one friend in town, and one at the lake in the summer. All three helped make life worthwhile, enjoyable, supportive.

This is the value of having a quality support system. It literally gives strength and boosts your immune system. I got through the teen years relatively unscathed thanks to my tiny support system. This is what many introverts do, whether in youth or adulthood.

The value of connection

A most fascinating research report concerning distance and connection was published by Bowen researcher, Andrea Maloney-Schara (1989). During the initial AIDS epidemic, the infected were dying rapidly. No treatment existed. Additionally, there was little understanding of a gay lifestyle—only judgment. Most gays had not disclosed their preference to their families for fear of total cutoff. So few had the energy or courage to make the double-whammy announcement when they were severely ill.

Bowen theory would predict that better-connected patients would do better physically and emotionally. Testing this hypothesis was the goal of the research, and it was proven true. Those who shared their reality, either naturally or with encouragement, survived longer despite the lack of proven treatment.

There was an unexpected result of the research. With the same big thinking of Bowen, Maloney-Schara thought to test family members of those who had received the news from their loved-one with AIDS.

She discovered a slight uptick in symptoms distributed throughout the family system. Symptoms could be physical, emotional, or social (such as drinking and law-breaking behaviors).

To me, it was as if a larger support group helped carry some of the burden, through their caring compassion. No one in the extended family was done in by their symptoms, despite the fear many had that "Mom and Dad will die of a heart attack when they hear the news!" This wasn't generally observed in the study.

I see it as almost mathematical, as depicted in figure 6.1. The squares over the patient's head in the first view represent the weight of the illness carried by the patient. In the second view, the weight becomes divided among a few supporters. The third view

shows the value of having a large support system. Each one

shows the value of having a large support system. Each one carries a fraction of the original weight. Of course the patient still carries the majority of the weight. This unique research fortunately will never be replicated with the AIDS population because good treatment now exists. But think of the value of this connection concept with any illness or stress.

We had the occasion to put Maloney-Schara's valuable Bowen-guided truths into practice for my dear husband, Dave.

On April 30, 2015, Dave was diagnosed with stage IV lung cancer. We were totally shocked as he was a healthy, non-smoker. He courageously asked what his prognosis was. The answer: "You have a 50 percent chance of making it 6 months."

Through years of practicing the Bowen theory, I had gradually cultivated a fantastic support system. Here are the ways friends and loved ones were able to pitch in:

1. Praying for us and asking others to pray for us. Whole

AIDS patient in total isolation died rapidly from the weight of carrying illness symptoms alone

Isolated patient with a few stressed friends, some of whom know others with AIDS. The added fear of traumatized supporters might have contributed to the quick demise.

AIDS patient with large involved support system survived longer though no AIDS treatment was available in the 80s.

FIGURE 6.1. The value of a support system

churches of varying faiths were asked to pray. We believe at least a thousand people prayed for Dave.

2. The week before his diagnosis, a friend called to say, "I'm so disturbed by all the people I know who are turning their back on Western medicine when they have cancer. Over a couple of decades, about a hundred of them have died that way." When Dave got his diagnosis, we were already primed to integrate both Western and complementary medicine.

3. Friends took Dave to receive his infusions so I could continue supporting us.

4. Knowing we were integrating Western and alternative medicine, many shared success stories of others. One epidemiologist spent ninety minutes on the phone sharing past and present research about successful cancer treatments.

5. Friends shared *The Truth about Cancer* series with us.

6. Two friends quickly volunteered to get us on lotsahelpinghands.org. Any time we had a need we sent only one request to reach our entire group automatically. Those who were available signed up for a time slot to serve the need. We loved this because the tasks were broken into one-hour commitments. We didn't want to burn out our support system, and only asked when we had a need. It was wonderful to be able to do so. Also, our friends didn't need to worry whether we needed help. They trusted us to reach out as needed.

7. One friend came to stay with us for a month during a very stressful time that included what Dave called the worst week of his life.

Support system strength survey

For years, I affirmed gratefully that the Bowen theory had enabled me to build a fantastic support system. I was inspired by the emotionally-mature people acknowledging they were emotionally well-connected with almost everyone in their family system, their neighborhood, their workplace, and organizational settings such as church, synagogue, temple, or mosque. Gradually my support system grew.

I decided to create a simple form called the support system strength (SSS) survey, so my clients could get clear on their support system.

You are welcome to complete this form yourself by downloading it at ibetherapy.com/relationshipresources.

The form provides space to indicate whether you can share or listen to real emotional content with each person on your support system. In other words, if you can share real emotional content or vulnerable things with a particular support person, indicate with an "S" for sharing. If you can listen, because the other person shares freely with you about themselves, indicate with an "L" for listening. And if you can do both sharing and listening with one person, indicate this with a "B" for balanced or both.

A week prior to consulting with EMDR therapists who were learning the iBE protocol, I offered the newly-developed SSS survey. I asked them to complete the form before the next meeting.

At our next consultation conference call, Robbie volunteered to share her results. She was able to listen to all the individuals on her generous list. But she indicated that she shared her own emotional reality with hardly anyone. This brought a rush of tears to her, as she realized what support she was missing! The exercise alerted her that she needed to begin sharing more of herself.

Honestly, in the beginning I had the same problem. Though I was interested in others, I assumed they weren't all that interested in me. That's why my support system was small. This was mostly owing to my lack of imagination on how things could be better. Bowen's concepts changed that for me.

When I totaled up my support system, I was not as overcome as Robbie. My surprise was not distressing, but astonishing. At first, my total was seventy-two people. Within a few days I had an aha moment. I'd omitted the wonderful women I served with at a spiritual camp for girls. I felt a close, trusting relationship with twelve friends there resulting from all the experiences we had shared for ten years.

Though I have a fantastic support system, there are times when difficulties mount, emotions are stirred up, and my cognitive faculties aren't totally in line. Many of us narrow our focus under similar circumstances. I can forget my support system. My clients have confided the same thing to me. They can feel totally alone, lonely, and sink into depression.

Remember your support system

At the first session for each client, I put their SSS survey in a plastic page protector and suggest they keep it in a handy place, such as in their nightstand. "Turn to it whenever you feel overwhelmed or lost." If you access the SSS survey at ibetherapy.com/relationshipresources you can do the same thing.

That is what the mature people did naturally. They were there for others as needed. But also, when they were faced with a conundrum, they could think of several people to turn to who were likely to give understanding, a listening ear, a practical suggestion, or even practical assistance. What a great resource!

In our busy lives, we can't always find a friend to help at the time we need the help. That is why I recommend growing abundance in your support system.

There is no need to rush or strain. As I mentioned earlier, three people worked pretty well for me initially. Perhaps I naturally added about three people a year to my system. This wasn't a conscious plan at first.

It is a reality that over time, people move, or get sick, or die. Misunderstandings may cause some relationships to end, peacefully or not. So there will be some degree of coming and going from the list. That is why it is a very good idea to keep adding to your system throughout life. If you live a long life, you could end up pretty lonely at the end if you don't cultivate new friends each year of your life.

It is a kindness to your support system to make sure you have more than one person on your list. A support system of one, whether a spouse or a friend, is severely limited. No one can meet all the needs of another. Small support systems will be stressed support systems, and thus, at risk for dissolution.

I don't remove anyone from my list. When a misunderstanding causes a distance, I send love from a safe distance and pray for peace and harmony. That way, in my heart I carry no hard feelings. If I do, I seek EMDR therapy. Life is too short, and as Lincoln brought to our attention the words of poet John Lydgate:

> You can please some of the people all of the time, you can please all of the people some of the time, but you can't please all of the people all of the time.

If someone wants to remove themselves from my support system, I take note, but I don't cut off from them. I patiently work to repair the relationship—as long as it takes.

Overcoming distance and cutoff

Bowen learned that for those who distance, the urge to get away is strong. For some of my clients, distance is their safe place. Thus, it doesn't work to pursue a distancer. It only makes them run away faster. And there's a word for that: harassment. People are super-sensitive to pursuit now. It has legal implications and can result in a restraining order.

A better approach when someone cuts off abruptly is to calmly express your wish to connect and reach understanding. Share that you would like to discuss a little sooner rather than a little later. And set your expectations as close to zero as possible.

Thus, you are not perceived as pushy and pressuring. The urge to get away eases just a bit in your brother, lover, daughter, or friend.

Many distancers are deeply conflict-avoidant. They feel much better in distance than in any confrontation. Others want to punish a wrong. Some hold grudges. If you can enter a curious state, wondering how long it may take to overcome the cutoff, you are in a good position.

Some gentle approaches to bridge the distance are presented below.

Bowen believed that less-mature people take longer to respond to the maturity-building strategies and principles described here. Reaching out with a light touch of contact, occasionally, is what my Bowen coaches recommended to me.

That way there is little to resist. The distancer can feel your calm interest in connection and sense your commitment to the relationship. Thus, you are sending a positive message, even if you don't use any of the words below in your touch. It's best to let your behavior demonstrate commitment to connection. Make the touches brief invitations, or little notes:

- I'd like to go for a walk with you soon. When is good for you?
- Hoping we could have tea or coffee together at our favorite park. What do you think?
- Send a card for birthday or holiday, with a warm message, but no request.
- Send a postcard when traveling: "Looking forward to doing something fun together next time I'm in town."

Depending on the situation, I may reach out with these touches once a month, or once or twice a year. Be prepared to deal with the pain of continuing rejection. Personally, I worked monthly for two years with one dear one. I found it rather grueling, but the cutoff was eventually overcome. Now the relationship has more life and closeness than ever before.

I know a monk whose cousin cut off from him when he entered the order of a church that was unfamiliar to the family. The cousin essentially disowned the monk. The monk did not match his cousin's cutoff. He reached out every year for Christmas and the cousin's birthday. After fifteen years of this, the cousin finally contacted him to warmly thank him for the ongoing love he expressed. The cousin asked if he could come to visit at the monastery. Yes! They had a joyous reunion and are now continuing a vital two-way relationship.

From a lifetime of practicing Bowen theory, I've observed that differentiated people find ways to express love, somewhat like the monk above. They are willing to see the other person's strengths, understand, respect, sympathize, care, listen to, take time with, and serve one another, which are all forms of love. Love has that magical ability to melt walls between people.

An old fable

Fables are great to illustrate concepts. This one reinforces this point about love.

It started with an argument. The Sun, the Rain, and the Wind were arguing about who was the most powerful of the three. They decided to have a competition. When they noticed a man walking along wearing a jacket, they decided it was the perfect test.

The wind said, "I can blow the jacket off him." The wind blew with all his might. But the man only zipped his jacket up tight and it stayed on. The wind finally blustered out and gave up in defeat.

The Rain confidently proclaimed, "You ain't seen nothing yet. Watch me go to work." The rain pelted the poor man with terrific force. But the man only pulled his hoodie on to protect his head. The Rain, too, had to give up and endure an exhausted failure.

The Sun quietly said, "Perhaps I can get him to take his jacket off." The sun patiently shone, and got warmer, and warmer. In time, the jacket dried off. The sun shone brighter. The man slipped his jacket off. He didn't need it anymore.

A real-life fable

Remember Beth in chapter 3, who shocked herself by attacking her future in-laws in the first act of violence she perpetrated in her life? Here is what she shared less than a month after she completed her two days of the iBE Workshop:

Connection

> You described how quickly I can make changes, and I'm finding that the family is changing, too, just two weeks later!

> I even called my grandparents to whom I haven't spoken in years. We had the best conversation we have ever had. And they asked to become my Reiki clients!

> Both my parents and grandparents have come to me for advice. When I gave it, they got quiet for a moment. And then they said, 'You're right.'

My client and I were both dumbstruck that this kind of change could happen just two weeks after a two-day workshop. Beth shared more that you will find in chapter 10 on balance and equality.

Life and connection

Building better connections is a good focus for progress in emotional maturity. Embark on a treasure hunt to find people who practice the maturity-building principles. Include some of them in your support system. A good support system can make it easier to cope with triangling, the next anxiety-binding mechanism which will be addressed in chapter 7.

. . . .

At a Glance: Choosing Connection and Patience

- When someone distances from you, invite them to reconnect a little sooner rather than a little later. Affirm that you value the relationship and want to understand.
- This process may take patience, because distancers feel most comfortable in distance. Offering an invitation to connect and setting your expectations about meeting as close to zero as possible, will eventually be successful if you are patient and persistent in your caring.
- When you want to distance, ask if you could try a brief conversation before you do so. Give room for the other person to express their truth. Ask for equal time to express your truth. Notice how this experiment went.
- Connection habits can give you a fantastic support system, inoculating you against stress. When you face a challenge, you can turn to many people for support or creative strategies to solve the issue.
- As you learn the qualities of emotionally-mature individuals, strive to invite more such people into your support system. Remember, support systems are for mutual benefit between equals.
- Respect your support system and take care to not burn out your supporters.
- Small support systems will be stressed support systems, and thus, at risk for dissolution. However, they can always be revived through the principles in this chapter.
- Differentiated people find ways to express love. They are willing to see the other person's strengths, understand, respect, sympathize, care, listen to, take time with, and serve one another, which are all forms of love. Love has a magical ability to melt walls between people.

Practical Tips

1. Complete the support system strength survey (found here: ibetherapy.com/relationshipresources). See how you might like to improve or add to your SSS.

2. Think about one or more people who have distanced themselves from you in the past. Try some of the steps in this chapter to rekindle a relationship you miss.

3. Think of someone you have distanced yourself from. Remember good memories you have with that person. Plan some light touches to revive the relationship. Schedule how often you wish to make a touch.

Chapter 7
Understanding Triangling—or Bringing in a Third

"Do not spread false reports."

Exodus 23:1

"If a wicked person comes to you with any news, ascertain the truth, lest you harm people unwittingly, and afterwards become full of repentance for what you have done."

Quran 49:6

"Be not apt to relate News if you know not the truth thereof."

79th Rule of Civility, George Washington

"Those who consider themselves religious and yet do not keep a tight rein on their tongues deceive themselves, and their religion is worthless."

James 1:26

Pop Quiz

T or F I have witnessed gossip or experienced being the target of put-downs, untruths, and cruel words by more than one person.

T or F I've been betrayed romantically.

T or F My parents worry about me a lot at certain times in my life.

T or F I find myself thinking about my own children more than I do about my spouse.

T or F When I'm angry with someone, I'm likely to let others know all about it.

Variations of triangling

Murray Bowen found that a two-person system is inherently unstable in times of stress. Human beings tend to bring in a third, which Bowen called triangling. Like a knee-jerk response, many automatically reach out to tell someone else about who upset them.

Because these people are operating on anxiety, they cannot be objective. Their blaming report will have some falsehoods. It is incomplete because the point of view of the other person is omitted. They conveniently omit any sense of their own contributing responsibility. If the listener passes the news on, the situation is amped up by another false report.

If we learned anything from the telephone game in childhood, we know messages passed on become distorted—fake news at the personal level. In a word, it is gossip.

There are other variations of triangling. Bullying is a style that combines triangling and conflict. It can be carried out through gossip (verbal abuse) that triangles in many people or through a violent gang attack.

The so-called lover's triangle is another style. When someone feels their needs aren't being met, they may turn to affairs.

Parents sometimes find it easier to focus on a child rather than the challenge with the spouse. Bowen called this style of triangling child focus. When this style occurs beyond the home setting, it can be called focus on a third.

All the opening quotes in this chapter deal with gossip, a common form of bringing in a third, fourth, or more persons. If our citizens could commit, individually, to avoiding this one anxiety-binding mechanism, how much more peaceful and effective could our national life become? It is a nice ideal. But because of human nature and anxiety, it is better to notice triangling when it occurs and learn in chapter 8 how to respond effectively to it.

Triangling examples

The basic triangling issue is a problem between two people that somehow gets deflected to or distracted from by adding at least a third individual. It postpones resolving the initial issue, sometimes indefinitely. Rather than resolving the anxiety, the anxiety subtly grows and spreads. As you will see in the next example, at times a volunteer comes into the triangle, uninvited.

Gossip

One evening, Aidan's big brother William teased him for crying to Dad about how hard his homework was. He just couldn't do it. The problem was between Dad and Aidan, but William invited himself into it.

Aidan still felt miserable the next morning at school when he saw Hannah arrive, wearing glasses for the first time and looking embarrassed. Aidan seized the opportunity to taunt her: "Ha Hah! Hannah! Ha Hah! Glasses!"

Hannah, who was shy, shrank away with tears rolling down her cheeks. And Aidan? He proudly marched around the classroom with two other giggling friends who witnessed the whole thing.

Kids can be cruel. If this situation didn't involve anyone else, we'd have a form of simple conflict. Since these involved a third, or a fourth, or more people, Bowen would call this pattern of behavior triangling—specifically, the gossip variation.

The lover's triangle

Many have experienced being dumped for another, and teens are not excluded from this misfortune. This is their grievous introduction into another form of triangling, the classic lover's triangle, aka the affair.

I once had the opportunity to spare my young son the predictable pain of an affair that he didn't see coming.

When Jacob was fourteen-years-old, he enjoyed the frequent phone calls of a cute eighth grade girl named Jillian. But I recognized the name as the girlfriend of his best friend, Rohan. I sat down with my son and acknowledged how much fun it is to receive the enthusiastic attention of a cute girl.

Then came the question. "If you had met and become Jillian's boyfriend first, and then introduced her to Rohan, how would you feel if she started calling Rohan a lot, and eventually they became tighter than you and her? "Not good," he replied with a sickened look on his face.

You've been friends with Rohan for a long time. He is very important to you, right?"

"Right," he affirmed.

"Would you want to risk losing that friendship for Jillian?"

"No way!"

"Then I suggest you be patient and wait. I guarantee you, their relationship will eventually end. Once their grief is over, and if you still really like Jillian, you can freely start up a closer relationship with her at that time."

"OK!" he sighed with a smile.

After our talk, Jillian and Rohan were tight for about one and a half years, including one break-up of a few months. In fact, they were so tight that Rohan rarely had any time for Jacob.

In their circle of friends, few liked Jillian because she dominated Rohan's time so much and showed little interest in them. Jacob learned two things from this: First, he didn't want to go out with Jillian once she was available. Second, when he eventually got a girlfriend, he would maintain his other friendships throughout the romance.

I noticed one other benefit my son learned through this experience. He became clear about his commitment to his friends. He also expanded his circle of friends, developing closer, more fun, and more supportive relationships with the other guys. This dedication expanded to Rohan once he became available again. Their friendship is now better than ever.

Betrayal by affair

My client Emily recently experienced double betrayal. She discovered her best friend and her husband were having an affair. This caused intense symptoms of panic. She had invasive images of the two together sexually. Her trust was shaken to the core. She had full-fledged PTSD.

When Emily discovered her former friend was not a true, committed friend, she immediately ended the friendship.

After eight years of sincere effort to improve their marriage, Emily and her husband were just in the process of deciding to end the marriage. They were planning how to inform the kids sensitively. Emily could not cut off from him because they needed to do a good job of co-parenting their dependent children together. And she needed to help her children navigate their feelings of betrayal and disgust about their father's behavior.

Emily is using EMDR to help her with all the traumatic aspects of this betrayal. She is no longer tortured by flashbacks or panic. Free from her intense emotional reactivity to her husband's choices, she is able to use her Bowen knowledge. She looks at each decision ahead considering the well-being of herself, the whole family, and their close network of friends.

She is taking clear and thoughtful "I" positions (see chapter 11). Emily is gaining inner strength and finding joy in her healthy relationships.

Child focus

The third variation of bringing a third person into a two-person relationship is child focus. It's easy to focus on a child who is more accepting and unconditionally loving than a challenging spouse. I call child focus the most popular and respected anxiety-binding mechanism in America.

Child focus involves shifting attention from the needs and problems of the marriage relationship to make a child's needs, problems, or talents the primary concern in daily life. Our American culture applauds the way we drive our kids to several extra-curricular activities per week, promoting as much perfection and success for our kids as humanly possible. Holiday letters and cards glow on about such activity.

It isn't wrong to do these things, of course. The activities are characterized by good intentions, love, and joy. But the wise question to ask is this: Where are we placing our priorities? Do we still go on dates or have good, long talks with our sweethearts? Do we take time encouraging our spouse and ourselves to practice good self-care of our own body, mind, and soul? If we work for a living, and we are making our children number one, is there enough time to do all the above?

The toll will be taken somewhere: on our relationship, on our body, mind, or soul. As Bowen observed, there will also be a toll on the children we adore.

Bowen found it didn't matter what style of child focus parents practiced. It could be a super-positive child focus: "You are such a prince/princess!!" It could be a negative child focus: "You are a real problem, kid. What's wrong with you?" Or it could be a lovingly worried child focus: "You are so vulnerable that we have to keep a very close eye on you and your symptoms."

Bowen concluded no matter how the child focus came off, it did the child in to a certain extent. As mentioned in chapter 1, the child focus pattern is the chief pattern practiced in the families Bowen studied—those with a young adult newly diagnosed with schizophrenia. You may recall Bowen didn't say child focus causes schizophrenia. If it did, we would have an epidemic of schizophrenia today.

Bowen did say that generations of child focus can produce schizophrenia. The speed of that result is due to the degree of stressors as the generations pass. The more the stress, the faster the result.

This is the danger of continuing a deep pattern of child focus, especially in the new millennium when stressors are intense. The good news is that anyone can consciously and thoughtfully change the pattern the moment they become aware of it. Chapter 8 offers practical strategies to help.

Do you, too, see child focus as widespread in our society today? The Bowen Center's recent Director, Dr. Michael Kerr, wrote on the Bowen Center website: "The current societal regression is characterized by an increased child focus in the culture."

This is a significant statement. I don't know how to evaluate his accuracy, but it is an interesting opinion with cautionary implications. I understand why he thinks this way. He was trained directly by Dr. Bowen, and has been paying attention to this growing trend during his many years of training and since Dr. Bowen's passing in 1990.

I have friends, relatives, and clients who are teachers. They are keenly aware of the intensity of the child focus pattern. It impacts their passion for teaching. Some have left the teaching field because of it. My nephew complained that he couldn't give students the grade they deserved without parents advocating for their child as if their future success depended on an A today. The parents are making the children much more important than the teachers. Parent-teacher relations are suffering as a result.

My cousin wonders how long he can last in the field he loves. He says he loves his time in the classroom. But the way parents power in to save their children from the consequences of their own poor work takes a great deal of joy out of his workday.

I was in high school five decades ago. My experience seemed idyllic in Minnesota then. The state valued education highly. Our taxes were high in part to pay for a great educational system. We had excellent schools and teachers. Thus, we enjoyed learning. And the parents backed up the teachers' decisions at least 95 percent of the time. We young people didn't interfere with the teachers. We gave them the same respect we (generally) gave our parents.

Understanding triangles and their effects

Imagine that in any two-person relationship there is a problem. Anxiety rises first, like a bubbling spring, in the one who initially notices the problem. If the anxiety is ignored by one or the other person, it generally bubbles through both.

If the two avoid solving the issue directly, the anxiety will continue gathering momentum, much like a brook, with little, growing streams spilling over onto others.

Figure 7.1 shows how Bowen illustrated triangles in child focus. The square and the top circle represent the father and mother, respectively. The solid, shaded circle is the daughter, relatively free from anxiety.

The dots represent anxiety building, like a bubbling brook, in the couple as they fail to address their problem.

Bowen and his researchers observed the triangle to be the basic building block of relationships. The third person can actually help stabilize the couple, as described below.

In Figure 7.2, anxiety spreads to the third person drawn into the range of the bubbling brook—in this case, the child. The couple's anxiety decreases as anxiety in the third person increases.

FIGURE 7.1. Triangles in child focus

Bowen identified interesting repercussions to triangling. The members of the couple feel a little more comfortable. The third person drawn in feels a little less comfortable, as he or she is now carrying added anxiety. However, if that person felt somewhat ignored prior to being drawn in, they may find the anxiety preferable to the boredom or loneliness.

Bowen said that in child focus, the child receiving the focus is done in to a certain extent by the additional anxiety they carry for their parents. It doesn't matter much whether the focus is positive or negative. And I want to make it very clear that the parents do not need to intend harm to the child. They generally do what they do with very little conscious awareness of their choices and the consequences.

A complicated triangle and its effect on a vulnerable child

Georgia's parents struggled in their relationship. Her father was a critical, bullying rager. The whole family lived in fear of him. Georgia watched her mother fearfully tiptoeing around him. To cope, Georgia's mom turned her main focus to

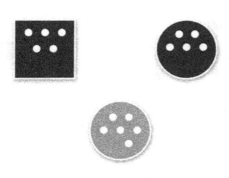

Georgia. She confided her troubles to her. Mom was very kind and attentive. Georgia really enjoyed this special status. She was relieved to have this positive experience in a family pummeled by verbal negativity.

FIGURE 7.2. Child focus triangle with anxiety spreading

However, the challenge for Georgia was that the anxiety-binding process inadvertently shifted Mom's anxiety to Georgia. Over the years, Georgia became increasingly plagued by symptoms of anxiety, depression, panic, and illnesses. Less able to cope with her mother's problems, she withdrew from her.

"The sad thing is that my mom turned from me to my sister as her support. That is when my sister started having problems."

Georgia's story is complicated. Many anxiety-binding categories were practiced in her distressed family. Her mother drew her in to become a parentified child, taking care of the mother. This will be described more fully in chapter 9 on the one up/one down pattern.

Child focus can shift as we saw with Georgia's mother. The target of any anxiety-binding mechanism can be shifted.

How can the focus be positive?

When parents make the child into a little prince or princess, many consider it positive. Some kids would even be jealous of such attention. The positive focus on the strengths, talents, and appeal of the child receives top billing.

If this is done in a balanced way, with parents able to give care to each other, the rest of the family, and to connections beyond the family, it's fine. The harmful aspect is that the adoration is primarily focused on one person. We all are aware of parents who see their children in this light. They have few interests beyond their child, and lack curiosity about you and your life.

Put yourself in the child's shoes. We might say positive focus is like being brushed with a feather over and over again—not when you want it, but when your parents want it. It is based on their need, not your real need.

The effect is somewhat like Chinese water torture. Drip, drip, drip. Brush, brush, brush. Focus, focus, focus. And the darling children with everything going for them develop symptoms.

Eye witness account: The high price to the child of positive child focus

Lisa shared that she could really relate to the children's book on dissociation she found on my waiting room table. She asked me to describe more what dissociation is.

I told Lisa most of us dissociate at times, such as when we are driving. "Aren't there times when you are unaware of what you are thinking and feeling as you cover the miles?" She agreed.

I explained further that some children learn to dissociate because they get the message that it is not OK to feel. Lisa could relate. For her, when she expressed her feelings, she felt increased pain. If she kept her emotion to herself, it was safer somehow. Like children who have a lot of early trauma, as a young child she learned to dissociate.

Dissociation may mean leaving one's body awareness. It may mean creating a fantasy life to gain a sense of control. The longer it continues, the more dissociation interferes with a person's relationships at home, at work, and throughout life.

Lisa agreed that her husband would complain when she zoned out: "You are not even listening to me! Will you please pay attention?" he often asked with frustration.

Sometimes she was able to recite the words he had said. At other times she couldn't, being unaware that her attention had drifted from the present. Often she would forget the immediate question, topic, or conversation, even while trying to respond to his communication.

This was frustrating for both of them. "I can't even talk to you!" he would announce in exasperation. What was once the safer option in the early family environment was wreaking havoc in her adult life.

I asked Lisa how she learned it wasn't OK to feel. She had to think about it for a while, because her parents were extremely loving and attentive. They placed their children at a high priority. No one would ever consider Lisa a victim of early trauma, as are most children who learn to dissociate in childhood. Lisa's parents cared so much. They followed a favorite parenting book as if it were an instruction manual. There is nothing harmful about that.

However, their reliance on the specifics of the parenting book resulted in many anxious, intense conversations between the two parents—often whispered directly in front of Lisa and her siblings. She watched them agonizing over what to do when a situation came up that wasn't in the instruction manual.

Lisa realized that whenever she or her siblings were hurt in some way, the parents went intensely overboard trying to solve their problem. She could see panic in her dad's eyes. He wanted so much to control the situation and protect his children.

"What are the options? Calculate. Think. Get it right. Oh, God, don't screw this up. I'm so distressed!" she imagined him thinking, as his nonverbal, but evident fear took over the room.

Lisa observed that he was distressing everybody. She did not want to be the cause or the focus of all that worry. She thought, "I can't stand this. I'm out of here." That is when she dissociated, whether she just left her body or left the room.

Her parents always remarked they couldn't believe that Lisa never, ever cried as a child. They reminisced that she was such an easy child. "My dad, particularly, always tells it as though I should be so proud of it. My mom remarks that she appreciated how easy I was, but always puzzled over my literally never crying. Over the years Mom kept asking why I never cried."

As we began to process this memory of her parents' style with EMDR, Lisa promptly repressed all her feelings. Dissociation. It took a while to help her get back in touch with her emotions. She measured her distress as a nine out of ten. She felt sad and lonely in the gut.

Because her parents had become so anxious, she felt there was no stable rock to lean on. Things became worse for her if she went to her parents. Even though they were trying to the nth degree, her needs weren't getting met.

Identifying normal focus versus too much positive focus

Child focus meets the parents' needs more than it meets the child's need. Unfortunately, in this case, the child was completely left behind and the parents didn't even recognize it.

All children need the attention of their parents. To avoid the kind of child focus that concerned Bowen, the key question for a parent to ask is: "What is my child's real need?"

Sometimes just calm listening will bring out that need. Sometimes it helps to let the child give words to describe what they want and how they are feeling. Ask the child, "What do you need now?" When you succeed in meeting the child's needs, you will soon hear, "I want to play!" This means they are in a healthy state, and ready to have fun with you. You know you managed to meet their need. And you may be reassured to learn how easy it is to meet kids' needs. They often just need sincere listening and comfort when distressed and play when happy.

By being attuned to these needs, you'll cultivate a strong relationship bond that will give stability and joy throughout life.

Negative child focus

Negative focus is a focus of a different feather. The sharpness of its quill is more intuitively obvious from the start. But still, negative focus can take subtle forms: undermining a child's confidence in himself, or worrying about her ability to take on new challenges or transitions.

It can also take the forms of unsubtle abuse: verbal and emotional name-calling, yelling, or violence.

Finally, the triangling pattern can combine both an affair and child focus—resulting in incest. This painful subject will receive more attention in my follow-up book devoted to going deeper into emotional maturity.

Triangling and schizophrenia

In his research, Bowen learned a fascinating insight about triangling that unfortunately has not been used to benefit all the people it could. As you will recall from chapter 1, he enlisted patients diagnosed with schizophrenia and their families to join the study. They naturally practiced child-focus on the child eventually diagnosed with schizophrenia.

As one or both parents began to focus on a child, they directed their own lack of differentiation on that child. In other words, parent and child didn't always know who was who. Remember the young college woman Bowen studied along with her family? Well into her twenties she didn't know her own feelings until her mother told her what they were.

These parents would find it easier to focus on the most vulnerable of their offspring rather than communicate with each other. The cycle would continue, causing decreasing emotional strength in one individual with each generation.

As you read before, Bowen's remarkable discovery after reviewing this generational pattern was this: Under circumstances of ordinary levels of stress, it can take up to ten generations of child focus to produce schizophrenia. Under extreme stress, it may take only three generations. Now you can see how this actually happens.

Bowen then drew a logical conclusion. It is not the mother who causes schizophrenia, but the continuing pattern of child focus. He worked to help the parents shift the pattern, to become more interested in and closer to one another. The result: he found that the son or daughter diagnosed with schizophrenia improved without added therapy. His strategy was that significant.

For some families, being able to shift the pattern was a big if. If they used only the child focus pattern without practicing any of the other ABMs (anxiety-binding mechanisms), they usually did not have the flexibility to change. But those who had some practice with the other ABMs could successfully shift, and the schizophrenic member would function far better.

This may be an ideal opportunity to remind you, my dear reader. If you are noticing that you may be practicing every anxiety-binding mechanism from time to time—especially when stresses are high—do not despair. Bowen found that this indicates your flexibility. He would give you an optimistic prognosis for improvement in your own growth and in the growth of your relationships.

Why is this? We develop more skills using the other ABMs. They may not be high level skills, but they are skills nonetheless. The practice we get by developing a wider variety of skills makes us more capable of developing additional skills. We're used to using our thought processes to create change.

I have found people who used multiple ABMs were more flexible, more willing, and more able to develop maturity-building principles once they understood the mechanics behind what was holding them back and creating their pain.

Consider some of the skills involved in the anxiety-binding mechanisms. In conflict, we are willing to point out what we don't like. In distance, we can change the subject when it's uncomfortable. In triangling, we distract from the key issues. Sometimes this is useful, as it buys time for thinking. In reciprocity, we can play either the one up or one down role.

From this range of options, it's not hard to start making conscious decisions about even more adaptive strategies. For instance, in a touchy conversation, you might want to directly and overtly buy time for thoughtful reflection: "Thank you for letting me know your views. Let me think more about these ideas and get back to you later."

When ready, you can speak one-to-one with each person involved in the original disagreement. This takes extra time but enables more flexibility with each person. It gives a better opportunity for understanding to grow. And it demonstrates the importance of each relationship like Bowen's emotionally-mature examples.

The child focus pattern may not seem very relevant to you if you are not a parent. However, when you look at the family you grew up in, who received the most focus? If it was you, ask yourself if sometimes you volunteered for the role. We can get used to our roles so they seem right in some way. At least they are comfortable. If you are ready to let go of the pattern, you could choose to stop volunteering for focus.

If you still find triangling is not very applicable to you, consider the national pastime of gossip.

A deeper look at gossip

Timothy Hallett, PhD, an associate professor in the Indiana University sociology department, defined gossip as "the unsanctioned evaluative talk about people who aren't present."

It is also useful to see what is not happening when gossip is in process. The gossipers are not sharing real emotional content about their own lives and their relationship with each other. They may feel a little closer, but can that kind of closeness last during the stresses of life?

Gossip is sad because it involves people dwelling on the weaknesses of others. We all have weaknesses. Thus, we are all vulnerable to gossip to a certain extent. From Bowen's point of view, gossip is an anxiety-binding mechanism. When feeling anxious, gossip makes many of us feel more comfortable, because at least for the moment we are not the one being criticized. Sometimes we even feel like we are one up when criticizing others.

Thus, it takes great strength to overcome these patterns. We need to find willingness to let go of the little comforts of ABMs such as triangling. By replacing ABMs with maturity-building principles (MBP) we'll gain the greater rewards of self-respect, self-confidence, and more real, more connected relationships.

How much gossip is happening in our culture today? So much that I will address it more deeply in my follow-up book. However, I will address Harvey Weinstein and the allegations of sexual abuse that are filling the papers.

Harvey Weinstein's sexually-abusive behavior had been featured in gossip tabloids for many years. He was a famous American film producer and co-founder of the motion picture company Miramax. Perhaps some people read about his abuse and heeded the warning for themselves. But his exploitation continued.

It was only after many women took strong public positions about his behavior that they achieved true safety from Weinstein's behavior. It happened when he was removed from his positions of power.

When the warning is true, gossip may be helpful. It may have empowered Weinstein's victims to take stronger action once actor Ashley Judd and others became brave enough to take a very public stand in 2017.

A sense of justice being served has now empowered many other victims as they continue to identify powerful abusers. The collective will is now bringing swift consequences—at last. Sigh.

Nonetheless, we still need to be thoughtful and see the big picture. There is a problem when the gossipy warning or accusation is false.

The following story reveals how a firestorm of gossip grew from one man's false report.

Retroactively repairing the damage of false gossip

Brad had made some poor choices financially for both his business and the family. His business partner, Harold, was upset that all was going south. Brad became extremely depressed and suicidal. To save his life, Brad's family hospitalized him.

At that point, Harold went to Brad's home offering help. The family thought he was repaying their past kindness. Previously, during a rough time for Harold, Brad and his wife had paid major bills for Howard's family.

Now Brad's wife, Michelle, was stuck in bed after leg surgery. Instead of helping, Harold seized all the business records. He declared to Michelle that Brad had hidden money in overseas bank accounts. Harold then started calling all their business contacts and even personal friends to gossip about Brad. He posed as the protector, saving everyone from Brad's alleged bad actions. Harold even said to Michelle, "Don't worry Michelle, I'll help you. I'll take care of you."

Some people believed Harold and never spoke to Brad again. Some people checked it out for themselves and learned the truth. Even Brad's wife had doubts, but through her own investigative work she learned that Brad was honest, and Harold was not. Overseas bank accounts were never a reality.

The people Harold talked to started gossiping among themselves. It became a tangled web, becoming more tangled as conversations flowed. Some people believed the worst, without question.

Harald's gossip reached Joe via the tangled web. Feeling doubt, Joe felt confused. He called his trusted friend Catherine. This seemed so unlike Brad. Catherine told Joe, "Yes, he is having difficulties. I don't know if the news is true. Now he can't defend himself. We will listen to him when he's not struggling for his life. But he is our friend. We will help him get well."

It was Christmas eve. Catherine took her family to the hospital dressed in Christmas attire. They sang Christmas carols for Brad and his fellow patients.

Brad was dumbfounded. So were the other patients. No one else had visitors on Christmas Eve. The family's sparkling faces and voices brought cheer to everyone. The other patients told Brad he was the luckiest man in the world. Brad has been eternally grateful ever since to Catherine and her family.

Brad felt guilt for his poor choices, but he knew he hadn't done anything deliberately to hurt anyone. He knew he didn't deserve the false charges. Brad later made amends for his mistakes to those who were willing to listen to him.

Michelle described this gossip as a catastrophic firestorm. It would have been worse had she decided to divorce Brad at that time. He could have been pushed over the edge. She knows her husband is a good person who would never intend do something wrong or illegal. That is why she stayed.

Brad became more introspective. He confided to Michelle that he used to be an angry person. "Anger can be empowering. It can engulf you and eat you up inside." He could work himself up to the point it was almost a high. Brad says he learned so much from all this that he maintains no anger against Harold.

As a result of his painful lessons with his former partner, recently Brad discovered he was able to apologize to someone after forty years. Long ago he had suddenly embraced a self-righteous, angry grudge with his friend, not to be revisited until a chance meeting. Both felt good about his sincere apology.

Questions inspired by the concept of triangling

I suggest thinking through your own answers to the following questions. Triangling is a very complex subject that affects us all. This book offers an introduction.

1. What benefits and pains can result from triangling?
2. When are we most at risk for triangling?
   a. For ourselves?
   b. From our loved ones?
   c. From outsiders?
3. How can we get back on track when we find ourselves caught up in the pattern of triangling?

Any time anxiety rises, triangles multiply. Under intense stress, they can become a catastrophic firestorm as Michelle put it. Emotionally-mature people address this in a way Bowen called detriangling. I look forward to sharing with you principles and strategies for dealing with triangles in chapter 8, Choosing Direct, Personal, Committed Relationships.

· · · ·

At a Glance: Understanding Triangling—or Bringing in a Third

- Triangles begin with a problem between two people and an increase in anxiety in the system.
- Triangles often are created automatically, with minimal conscious thought.
- Thus, they are not communicated with clarity or integrity.
- Triangles sometimes remain secret for a while.

- The third (or more) person(s) brought into the triangle diffuses the anxiety from the original two members.
- The increased anxiety in the new member(s) may be received as a positive if they were previously ignored.
- Child focus is a prevalent form of triangling in today's society.
- Child focus can be positive or negative—both can cause damage.
- Generations of child focus results in schizophrenia in three to ten generations.
- Triangles can increase anxiety and cause pain.
- Gossip is a prevalent form of triangling.

Practical Tips

1. If you have a problem with one person, ask if anyone else is indirectly involved—for instance, have they discussed the problem with anyone else, or are they influenced by anyone else regarding the problem the two of you are having? If so, a triangle is involved. If this is the case, and if it's appropriate, think of how you might improve the relationship with the third person as well as the first. Work to improve each relationship individually.

2. Do you recognize yourself practicing child focus? Try researching yourself. Notice when you shift into child focus. Track how much time you practice focusing on a child, for each incident. Whom do you tend to focus on most? What concerns prompt the focus? What are the possible outcomes?

3. Do you find yourself tempted to stray from a commitment by having a flirtation or an affair? Research yourself to identify when you feel this urge. How strong is the urge? What stressors or needs are prompting this strategy to meet the needs in this way? Who could be hurt by your actions? What might happen if you express your needs calmly, in a vulnerable way?

4. Do you gossip? If so, catch yourself next time and think about the potential consequences. Does it serve a positive or negative purpose for you? For the other person?

5. Have you been a perpetrator or a target of gossip? Confirm the truth of the situation with yourself (and others, if necessary). Then take action to repair the understanding of the facts with those who will listen.

Chapter 8
Choosing Direct, Personal, Committed Relationships

"Jesus said unto him, thou shalt love the Lord thy God with all thy heart, and with all thy soul, and with all thy mind. This is the first and great commandment. And the second *is* like unto it, thou shalt love thy neighbour as thyself. On these two commandments hang all the law and the prophets."

Matthew 22:37-40

"We have to recognize that there cannot be relationships unless there is commitment, unless there is loyalty, unless there is love, patience, persistence."

Cornel West

"When confronted with a challenge, the committed heart will search for a solution. The undecided heart searches for an escape."

Andy Andrews

Pop Quiz

T or F   I am worthy of committed relationships.

T or F   I am afraid to commit in a relationship due to all the bad relationships I've seen.

T or F   I can see how I volunteer to be the center of attention, and how it hurts me sooner or later.

T or F   I can see ways I was influenced to believe that making children number one is ideal.

T or F   When someone gossiped, I have said, "I don't want to gossip. Let's change the subject."

The complexity of triangles

Human relationships are complex and often stressful. As you read in chapter 7, Bowen in 1978 posited that a two-person emotional system is inherently unstable in the face of stress, and a third person often is triangled-in to create stability. Jenny Brown, PhD, a social worker and Bowen family systems therapist from Sydney, Australia and author of *Growing Yourself Up* (2012) simply calls triangling bringing in a third.

Triangles come in three common patterns: gossip, affairs, and child focus. Gossip is a method for bringing in a third. The third person can be brought into the situation to enable one of the distressed members to express their frustrations and to gain sympathy. Or they may simply wish to remove the discomfort of being alone with the other person.

We may have the sad experience of love triangles to contend with. Or we may have experienced the detrimental effects of child focus.

If you are unaware of the concept of triangling, your relationships might seem so complex and mysterious that you don't know what to do to bring balance. There may even be hidden triangles that cause confusion and frustration.

If you want to improve your relationships, understanding the challenges of triangles is important. This chapter will help you to look more closely at triangles to help you untangle their effects. It will help you understand what committed, direct relationships are about, and how to form them.

Reversing the triangling move

My wonderful mother-in-law provided the quote in the last pop quiz question above, "I don't want to gossip. Let's change the subject." I loved her for it. Instantly, I knew this was a safe family to be in. She and my father-in-law, through their strong, principled leadership, made it safe.

Murray Bowen was interested in how emotionally-mature people handle triangling when they detect it. He found they respond along these lines:

- I go directly to the individuals involved, one at a time.
- I reach out to connect, one-to-one.
- If there is gossip about me, I work to repair any misunderstanding.
- I don't choose sides, and work to be as neutral as possible by understanding the others from the biggest perspective I can.

Another said:

- Sometimes I might do unexpected things in a creative or even playful spirit.

Bowen called this practice of turning triangles into more personal, one-to-one relationships detriangling. To me, all the actions described by the emotionally-mature individuals constitute commitment to a personal relationship, as well as commitment to principles which keep the relationship trustworthy.

Detriangling does not require major commitment. It simply values a one-to-one, direct, and personal relationship with each person you interact with, whether that be a neighbor, coworker, relative, friend, or beloved.

Whether we call it detriangling or working for more direct relationships, the following example achieves the goal of improved relationships. A client named Brandy shared how she helped herself and her sisters detriangle from their mother's gossip.

Brandy grew up with four sisters. They always had challenges getting along. Their mother frequently repeated to Brandy, "You should hear what the others said about you."

Finally, Brandy got the idea that this was not just happening to her, but her mother was repeating gossip to all her sisters. She had a hunch Mom was a major factor in their sisterly disharmony and the fact that they hardly spent any time together. So, she invited her sisters to participate in an experiment.

Brandy called her mother for their regular phone call. She didn't let Mom know her other sisters were already on the phone using the conference call feature. Pretty soon her mother started fomenting problems by claiming Sister A had disparaged Brandy about her weight, and Sister B had criticized her kids' behavior.

After a few more minutes (enough time for all the sisters to have been blamed for something) the sisters spoke up: "Mom, what you said wasn't true. We want you to stop gossiping and creating problems between us. We love each other and want to be real sisters from now on."

It worked! Their mother adapted to their united front, and to their clear, firm communication of the behavior they would no longer tolerate.

Averting gossip in a mature way

Because the emotionally-mature people Bowen observed valued personal, well-connected relationships, they tended to have less triangling problems to begin with. Their proactive efforts were sometimes an inoculation against triangling (though surely not always!). At least their efforts to connect better may have helped to soften the fallout from gossip.

When someone knows you well and they hear false gossip about you, they will stick up for you and say, "I know Jill, and

I know for a fact that she wouldn't knowingly hurt anyone. I believe there has been a misunderstanding here, and I recommend you go directly to her to resolve it. I wish you well in your relationship with her."

If an emotionally-mature person got wind of gossip about them, they may go to each person relevant to the issue. They might say, "I heard this said about me, and want to let you know my perspective."

They would clarify their own views, feelings, opinions, or values related to the issue. They would invite the person to "please check with me if you hear any gossip about me. I appreciate your coming to the source instead of getting second-hand info, and I will do the same for you."

However, if someone gossips to us, we can step out of it by directing them to the person they have a problem with. In my mind, I visualize them together, resolving the issues.

In the examples above, the people involved are practicing well-defined boundaries.

What happens to triangles over time

Systems of three or more people become systems of interlocking triangles. Anxiety and messages can swiftly move through a system of triangles, so triangles are very important to understand in learning to manage stress. With social media, the multiplication of triangles can be almost unlimited.

It may seem contradictory to triangle-in others to reduce stress, because in many ways this process increases stress and anxiety for others. But trianglers feel an immediate, short-term reduction in their anxiety. This strongly rewards their activity, creating a continuing behavior pattern.

Over time, however, use of anxiety-binding mechanisms increases overall anxiety. Through generations, it causes a regression of functioning for vulnerable individuals in each generation (known as intergenerational transmission process). Thus, triangles pose a problem of short-term gain and long-term loss.

Gaining a neutral perspective

Triangles fluctuate and change predictably

Each one of us was born into our first basic triangle including self, Mother, and Father.

People with higher levels of differentiation can be flexible in their triangles and maintain hold of their principles and their selves despite the ebb and flow of triangles.

People with lower levels of differentiation tend to become set in their triangles for long-term patterns. They find change more difficult yet even more valuable to achieve. They work hard to fuse with people, yet the resulting intensity makes life so hard.

Triangles tend to operate with two people being closer, and with one on the outside of the triangle. In times of calm, the close position is favored. In times of intensity, the outside position is preferred. Alliances can change.

The flow of closeness and distance in relationship triangles can be tracked. If you observe the process like a researcher in your own family and identify your own part, you have a great opportunity. Once you recognize triangling occurring, you can start changing your part thoughtfully, based on Bowen theory and your best introspection about your family or relationship system. It may not be easy, but you will gain inner strength from the process.

Bowen was extremely encouraging about such efforts. He said, "Microscopic progress is huge," and he meant it. If a person with low differentiation increases their level of differentiation just a little, it reverses a natural trend of regression. The benefits will help that person as well as those in triangles with him or her.

I find this one of the most optimistic things about Bowen's theory.

Someone practicing a researcher mindset, as Bowen encouraged, will be curious to track when and how the alliances change. When you become curious, you are on your way to neutrality. It is a sign you are also gaining flexibility.

Neutrality in a relationship triangle means the ability to remain unbiased by emotion or prejudice when thinking about the other two members of the triangle. One of the best ways to gain neutrality with both sides of a triangle is to meet one-to-one with the other individuals in the triangle.

Someone who is neutral can look at a situation for what it is, considering why the other person might have the feelings and beliefs they do. They can step outside of themselves, giving others the benefit of the doubt and leaving room for people to think differently.

People striving for neutrality want to look at each relationship in this way. Some relationships will be more challenging than others. But the effort is a worthy one.

Neutrality opens the door to truth and compromise

The more neutral we can become, the more we become open to truly listening to others. It is useful to detach, as much as possible, from our own perspective. It is not necessary to permanently leave behind our own view. But unless we can put it aside, we can't be open to the truths of others. Such a practice of neutrality enables creative compromises to arise that could match the truths of both people.

Changing others by changing yourself

Gossip is ubiquitous. It is ironic in this culture that gossip is such a way of life that it permeates reality TV, news, sports, and magazines. At the same time, the fear of commitment has increased to a level I never saw forty years ago. Both are indications of societal regression in our overall level of emotional maturity.

This gives you an idea of how challenging it can be to go against the grain, and try to bring more emotional reality, more personal sharing, and more life into our relationships.

People will often resist your effort at one-to-one communication. Bowen observed that they get "twitchy" as you do this. Doing so surely keeps things from being boring, and helps relationships to go deeper. But it requires a little more vulnerability. And it may require patient persistence and lots of deep breathing.

As Brené Brown (2015) discovered, "Vulnerability is about having the courage to show up and be seen when we have no control over the outcome."

Brown made a powerful point: we have no control over the outcome. The emotionally-mature do not control the outcome any more than less-mature people do, despite the latter's intense efforts to do so.

Showing up and being vulnerable

It is not easy to share one's truth. Sometimes someone does something to us that hurts. If we share our feelings about what happened, we risk being hurt, or discounted again.

However, without sharing them we risk missing a beautiful opportunity to deepen and strengthen the relationship. When this happens, the relationship becomes a more treasured and trusted friendship, whether it is with a relative, coworker, colleague, or neighbor.

I have found it useful to take risks with people, within limits. I'm willing to be vulnerable with three sincere efforts. However, if treated with anxiety-binding categories (such as conflict, control, ignoring, gossip, or one upping), after three occasions I draw a line. To me, it is three strikes and you're out. I don't mean the person is out, but I will keep a distance when my vulnerability isn't appreciated.

Again, Bowen advised people to have a researcher's mindset. Researchers want to observe truth. They are not trying to control it. They seek neutrality to learn the most truth.

One way my Bowen coaches cultivated neutrality in me was by giving me this cautionary note regularly: "Set your expectations as close to zero as possible." To me this means to do my best to practice theory and principles well, and let go of expectations of how the other person will respond.

Will that mean that I truly have no expectations? Rarely. However, Bowen's guidance helps me direct less anxious attention to how the other person responds to me and instead focus more on playing my own role to the best of my ability.

How to be safer from affairs

Commitment to your most cherished principles and relationships helps you to resist affairs, no matter how temptingly the opportunity greets you.

My husband told me stories of young women trying to hit on him at work. They apparently were attracted to his gentle, kind way. We were surprised to learn that the fact he was in a committed marriage made him even more attractive. They strategized he was a safer sexual partner.

He described the challenge of coworkers who wore low-cut tops flirting with him and asking him to go out. Their pursuit was not just assertive, but aggressive, as he shared in this common scenario, repeated with different women from time to time:

Woman: Hey, want to come over and have some fun tonight?

David: No thanks, I'm married.

Woman: No one needs to know.

David: But I'm happily married.

Woman: Who can it hurt if no one knows about it?

David: Look, I've always been able to look down the road and see how much pain it would cause everyone involved.

Dave said that his last comment was like dumping an ice-filled barrel of Gatorade over the woman's head. She finally got it, and never propositioned him again.

My sweet husband communicated clearly with each woman and also with me. Intuitively he knew how to communicate with both parts of the triangle. I was proud of him for the way he handled the temptation. My faith in his trustworthiness was so strong that when he became a massage therapist working on women and men who were unclothed under their sheets, I had no moment of fear or jealousy.

David and I cultivated commitment from the time we started discussing marriage. We asked our minister for a copy of the marriage vows. Though we were living a hundred miles apart, we started our daily phone call by repeating a vow to one another.

Our enthusiasm about this practice created a deep connection and trust in one another. In my first marriage, I had been betrayed. I had a deep need for safety in my next marriage. We practiced this for some months before I knew David was the right person for me and agreed to marry him. Once I agreed, we forgot about the vows until the day of our wedding. But the vows were still beautifully meaningful since we had given them so much of our attention.

After the wedding, we agreed that if we ever had a difficulty we couldn't resolve together, we would read our vows. For that purpose, we had placed them in a lovely frame and hung them conveniently in our bedroom. This was a wonderful strategy. By the time we finished the reading, we were lifted out of our own limited viewpoint into the principles and ideals that meant so much to both of us. In a sense, we recommitted to our values. This made it easy to recommit to the greatest good for both of us.

The process worked well. But occasionally, we decided we also needed to see either an individual or a couples' counselor. We had a wonderful marriage. I wouldn't say it was easy. We were both very strong-willed people. Both of us were the oldest among our siblings. We were used to being somewhat in charge. We worked for understanding, loving connection, and equal partnership with all our hearts, minds, soul, and strength. Hence, we called it a spiritual marriage.

When there is a lack of trust

What can you do if you are not fortunate enough to have a trustworthy partner? Perhaps you have suffered a transgression and betrayal. Or you've observed your partner flirting or overdoing interest in attractive people.

The question to consider is this: do you have basic trust of this partner? Does he or she acknowledge the transgression? Is there sincere remorse and willingness to step back within the physical and emotional boundaries of commitment? If so, the trust can be rebuilt but it will require sincere effort.

Forgiveness by the person wronged will be needed at some point. But it does not work to demand forgiveness prematurely. An excellent resource for this is *Forgive for Good* by Fred Luskin, PhD. He has researched a nine-step process for forgiveness. Guess what the ninth step is? Yes, that is when forgiveness comes.

The pain of betrayal can be traumatic. One or both persons may benefit from EMDR to overcome flashbacks and other intense symptoms. Working with a couples' specialist is advised.

This self-help book can help you prevent betrayals. But if a betrayal has occurred, it is generally beyond the scope of a self-help book. Recommended options include an EMDR couples' specialist, Bowen therapist, Gottman therapist, emotionally-focused therapist, or iBE therapist.

A benefit of commitment

Making a commitment involves caring deeply enough that you want to be there for your friend or loved one to the best of your ability. This does not mean doing everything the person wants you to do.

Commitment doesn't mean slavery. It means doing your best, being true to yourself as well as to your friend to the best of your ability. You want them to be able to count on you to a high degree, and mutually, you want to be able to count on each other.

When a friend shares something personal with you, commit yourself to being trustworthy with that information.

Here is one way that commitment can bring more joy and strength to life. My friend Therese shared a story of growing up in Iraq as a Chaldean Christian. She was having a difficulty with her mother's strictness.

Her father approached her to discuss the difficulty with her. I'll save the details for the future book but want to give you the overview of his approach now. He made it clear he was in full support of his wife, respecting her needs and standards. Yet he also made it clear he was a great believer in Theresa's strengths and feelings.

Theresa could see that he valued both her and her mother deeply. She left the conversation feeling like the three were a team, and she belonged.

As you connect with each member of your family, work, or neighborhood system (or as many as you can) you are building your own team, your network of personal relationships.

Triangle challenges

Georgia's parents struggled in their relationship. Her father was a bullying rager. Her mother lived in fear, tiptoeing around him. To cope, Georgia's mom turned her main focus to Georgia. She confided her troubles to her. She was very kind and attentive. Georgia really enjoyed this special status.

However, the challenge of child focus for Georgia was that the anxiety-binding process inadvertently shifted Mom's anxiety to Georgia. Over the years, Georgia became increasingly plagued by symptoms, including anxiety, depression, panic, and physical conditions. She became less able to cope with her mother's problems and withdrew from her.

"The sad thing is that my mom turned from me to my sister as her support. That is when my sister started having problems."

Georgia's story is complicated. Many anxiety-binding categories were practiced in her family. Her mother actually drew her in to become a parentified child, taking care of the mother. This will be described more fully in chapter 9.

Child focus can shift as we saw with Georgia's mother. The target of any anxiety-binding mechanism can shift.

. . . .

Lane came for help because of workplace trauma. She had been the target of two supervisors who used bullying tactics. After Lane left the abusive workplace, she learned from coworkers that the supervisors simply shifted their behavior to others. Their practice was to choose one person at a time to denigrate and micro-manage. One at a time the stressed employees quit, until none were left. (This is a sign of extreme dysfunction at a workplace. The workplace could be described as extincting. Families can go extinct as well.)

Once the employees were gone, the most powerful supervisor turned her cruelty on her fellow bully.

Anxiety-binding categories have force to them. They are fed and driven by anxiety. Just because one target folds, the anxiety doesn't go away. It seeks another target.

Keeping helpful child focus appropriate

Child focus is the most natural thing in the world when you have a child with a diagnosis, whether it is polio, diabetes, autism, cancer, depression, panic, or anxiety. Of course, it is necessary and reality-based to attend to the increased need or danger.

The question is, can we maintain balance, equality, connection, commitment, and understanding as we increase the child focus only to a necessary degree?

Wilma Rudolph's (1977) mother Blanche assisted her to get the necessary treatments for her polio and other illnesses. But she did not overly worry about her daughter or shift her own anxiety onto Wilma. Wilma frequently said, "My doctors told me I would never walk again. My mother told me I would. I believed my mother."

Sometimes the most valuable role a parent can play is to give the child a positive, yet balanced view of themselves.

Wilma Rudolph became the first American woman to win three gold medals at once in the 1960 Olympics.

If you have a child with a need of some kind, ask yourself: "Am I doing this step for my needs or my child's needs? Does my child really need me to do this for him or her?"

Sometimes the answer will be "Yes!" and sometimes it will be "No." To overcome child focus, it's a very good question to ask.

Wise triangling may be useful

Sometimes it is wise to consciously create a triangle. This may sound strange, but when there is a lack of safety, the strategic use of a third (or more) person as a witness can inspire the unsafe person to behave better.

Unsafe people tend to do their damage when they have privacy. I learned this principle when I discovered my friend Meredith had been stealing from me. It took a while to get over my denial, but when I saw one of my belongings among hers and started to pay attention to the mileage when she borrowed my car, I could see she was stealing, and was using the car more than she told me.

So, I asked a noble friend, Patricia, to serve as a witness while I confronted Meredith. We got together and I explained that Patricia was there because I knew she would never gossip about our conversation. She would simply be a silent witness.

I told Meredith the facts I had noticed. She listened calmly. Patricia's quiet presence probably increased the calmness of the discussion. Meredith didn't really admit to anything but didn't contradict anything either. She understood I would no longer be lending her my car. There was no more stealing after that.

Had Patricia not been present, it is likely that Meredith would have reacted with more emotion and sensitivity. She could have used any of the anxiety-binding methods: criticizing me or storming out of my home. Things could have gotten out of hand.

Sexual harassment

Sexual harassment is generally committed in private. Thus, it is not possible to invite a witness to be present. But since we have cell phones, its recorder can serve as your witness. It is legal if you are open about it. You can record your message in this way:

> It is three p.m. on Thursday, December 14, 2017. Present in this room are myself, Dana Terrell, coworker Mary Jones, and John Doe, supervisor. Any of us can ask to have this recording stopped at any time.

You can use this in a situation when someone is trying to harass you sexually. After you record this introduction, you can add, "Is there anything else you wanted to say at this time? I want to make sure we have a clear understanding of one another."

Since harassment and even sexual abuse are done in secret, it is very easy for the perpetrator to deny it. But if you let the abuser know you have a right to record the incident, the balance of power can shift in your direction. It is advisable to seek legal counsel about applying this idea in your state.

Workplace abuse

I've shared this conscious triangling idea with many clients dealing with abusive or harassing bosses. My client Jennifer shared the results of using it with a new female boss who blew up and exploded at her just three months into her new job.

She'd received excellent feedback from coworkers prior to an incident and knew her boss was off with her shockingly abusive comments. On the first occasion, she wasn't ready for the boss's behavior and was stunned silent.

On the second occasion, she was ready. When the boss shut the door again for a private conversation, Jennifer calmly opened the door. She brought out her cell phone and cued up the audio recorder. While doing so she said, "I'd like to record our conversation because I don't want to let any details slip through the cracks."

This time her boss was "as nice as can be!"

Workplace abuse and sexual harassment will receive more attention in my follow-up book.

Creativity, humor, and triangles

It is easy to feel very serious about triangles. Sometimes handling them seriously is completely appropriate. However, there are times when humor can quickly diffuse triangles. My mother specialized in this.

One day Mom had to cope with my teen mood. I was very angry about something. She could nearly hear me huffing and puffing, about to blow the house down and everyone in it. With witnesses present, she said, "Dana, I beg of you one thing."

I was all ears immediately. She never begged for anything.

"Please, (long pause for effect) whatever you do—don't smile."

I burst out laughing and the mood was gone.

Sometimes I've suggested to clients that they shift gears on one of their entrenched patterns by using props to bring a little lighter awareness to the pattern. This usually requires an advance agreement on the part of both partners to work well. That way both can enjoy the spirit of creative fun.

For instance, if someone tends to micromanage or nitpick family members, the partner can playfully pull a magnifying glass out of the junk drawer, wink and say, "Will it help to use this?"

The partner who loves to do back-seat driving from the front seat could be offered a referee hat. "Will this hat make your job easier?" Think of how refreshing a little humor could be for any children in the car!

To prepare for this fun, the parents could go shopping together for that prop. You might even find things to decorate it with from a craft store. The time spent cooperating on ways to shift the patterns is already softening the pattern you've been stuck in.

Thinking strategically about triangles

Bowen advised people to keep the phenomenon of triangles in mind. If you have a problem with one person, ask yourself: Is there a triangle involved here? If there could be, you may need to resolve something individually with each member of the triangle.

I called one of my relatives regularly but didn't get a call back. It seemed very strange. My Bowen coach said, "Often the spouse serves as a gatekeeper. How is your relationship with the spouse?" I said, "Not that great."

She advised, "If you work on your relationship with the gatekeeper, I think you will have no problem getting your relative to call back."

I found this to be absolutely true. I had no problem after working on the relationship with the spouse. The bonus is that now I enjoy two meaningful relationships.

This story exemplifies the value of looking deeper than the relationship between my relative and me. I had to look for the triangle. Things are sometimes more complex than they appear.

When we are unconscious of triangles, they can be a mysterious, frustrating, or even traumatic force leaving you feeling powerless or hopeless. Try becoming more conscious about the triangles in your life. Experiment with efforts to make relationships more direct.

If it is a great challenge, which triangles truly can be, please consider seeking help rather than giving up. When you can't overcome the challenge, it is useful to acknowledge that your trust of this person is limited. You can choose to withdraw from someone who triangles habitually. It is a sign of a less-mature person.

I wish you growing confidence in addressing and defusing triangles. May you transform triangles into personal relationships with even a little more sense of close commitment. You will find people trust you more. Whether the increase in closeness is microscopic or huge is not so important. Any improvement is positive progress and a significant shift from past stuck patterns. Your example will help the current relationship system, and future generations, to be more flexible as well.

. . . .

At a Glance: Understanding Direct, Personal, Committed Relationships

- Relationships are improved through direct communication and commitment, setting clear boundaries, and avoiding gossip.

196 When I Do Relationships So Right How Do They Go So Wrong

- Over time, triangles increase anxiety, and lead to intergenerational and societal regression.
- Emotionally-mature people commit to practicing their principles equally with all, and to thinking with the biggest perspective they can to gain neutrality about each person's position.
- Neutrality can be used to reveal the truth in a confusing triangle by remaining open to others' perspectives.
- Adjusting your one-to-one relationships using Bowen principles can lead to changes in others and improved relationships.
- Consistent commitment can rebuild broken trust.
- Child focus is a prevalent form of triangling in today's society.
- Wise triangling helps when dealing with unsafe others.

Practical Tips

1. When you have a problem with someone, ask if a third party might be playing a part.
2. Be sensitive to the concerns others express directly to you regarding your relationship. This helps to prevent their feeling so frustrated they get an urge to gossip.
3. Practice focusing on your child's real needs, and balance that focus with attention to your partner and others who rely on your committed presence.
4. When someone shares personal information with you, commit yourself to being trustworthy with that information.
5. Plan how you want to handle it if you hear someone sharing something negative or vulnerable about a third person. Consider my mother-in-law's clear boundaries: "I don't want to gossip. Let's change the subject."
6. Practice neutrality, or balance, by trying to see the strengths and weaknesses of each person involved in a challenging situation. Commit to not taking sides unless it is important enough to you to take an "I" position (see chapter 11).

7. Communicate your neutrality to avoid choosing sides with others in the triangle.

8. Neutrality can also be cultivated by using humor or creativity for stuck triangles. Be sure it is inclusive humor, rather than sarcastic humor which feels rejecting and does not help.

Chapter 9
Understanding One Up/One Down Reciprocity

"Give not Advice without being Asked & when desired do it briefly."

68th Rule of Civility, George Washington

"Any time I am in resentment, I am not taking care of myself. I am blaming someone else for something I need to do."

Al-Anon sayings

"The higher the expectations, the lower the serenity. I try to keep my boundaries high, my expectations low, and my heart open."

Anonymous

Pop Quiz

T or F I sometimes ask for help habitually, though I may not have needed it.

T or F I'm quite certain I know what is best for certain other people.

T or F I am responsible for my own happiness. I don't give others that responsibility.

T or F I tend to jump "all in" to any challenge. Others take advantage of that and slack off.

T or F I find it hard to choose goals and stick to them.

About the phrase one up/one down

Bowen and his researchers noticed a fourth and final pattern of coping with stress or anxiety in human relationships. They called it overfunctioning/underfunctioning reciprocity, because Bowen preferred terms that were descriptive and neutral.

Others since then, such as Jenny Brown, PhD (2012) have called it one up/one down. Both terms are an attempt to describe a pattern similar to codependency, but broader. I often use one up/one down for simplicity. I sometimes add the word reciprocity to convey this is not a rigid pattern, but one that can seesaw between one inclination and the other.

My goal is to help you gain more neutrality about this complex pattern, to reduce its ability to bother or control you or control others due to your actions or attitudes. Let me clarify that being neutral doesn't mean to tolerate or ignore the problem. It means to hold on to your calm reasoning and calm feeling to respond to reciprocity effectively when it happens.

In chapter 10 you will learn positive attitudes and strategies for responding to various attempts to overfunction or underfunction, or go one up versus one down.

What is overfunctioning/underfunctioning?

Simply defined, overfunctioning/underfunctioning reciprocity is when one person is doing less than their share (the underfunctioner, or one down person) often because they know the other will make up for it (the overfunctioner, or one up person).

Some may wonder if the one up/one down pattern refers to people who try to assuage their insecurities by putting their partner down or judging them constantly. That is not Bowen's or Brown's basic meaning of one up/one down. Putting down and judging adds the conflict style, with its criticism and control, to the one up/one down anxiety-binding mechanism

(ABM). When ABMs are combined, the anxiety and the problems are multiplied. This chapter discusses one up/one down as a separate pattern.

In Bowen theory, the term reciprocity means that the people practicing this pattern are moving between overfunctioning and underfunctioning like a see saw. They can go up or down but find it hard to be together in an equal posture.

Those who go one up, when stressed, naturally comfort themselves by doing too much, being the superman or superwoman, or the servant of all, taking care of all, nurturing all.

There is nothing wrong with competence, selfless nurturing, and care. We all need it and we all feel good when we give it. But when we no longer have a choice about doing or caring, when we feel we must do it, or we do it out of subtle anxiety or fear rather than based on calm reasoning about real needs, we risk becoming a habitual workaholic, superhero, or caregiver at the expense of our own well-being.

Bowen calls this person the overfunctioner while much of the psychology world calls them the codependent. Both refer to the same concept. Going one up is a problem because in time it puts strain on the overfunctioner and his or her relationships.

It is particularly problematic when a child becomes an overfunctioner. This is called a parentified child. The child doesn't have the maturity to fill the role. They know it at some level and feel the stress.

The flipside is the person Bowen called underfunctioning, who feels natural comfort in relaxing, letting go, and avoiding stressors a bit too often by finding other things to do that are easier or more appealing.

Of course, there is nothing wrong with relaxing and letting go. We all need to do that. But when we choose to let go rather than take up our responsibilities in life, we are going to have a problem. Whatever we do too little can become a kind of avoidance, procrastination, or fear. We get in a habit of being one down. The risk is to turn to addictions to obliterate the bad feelings that accompany the one down position.

Overfunctioners are stressed in different ways and may turn to addictions as well. My client Vanessa was surprised to learn that her workaholic husband spent a good share of his evening at the office using pornography instead of working.

This is a case in point that we can overfunction in one realm while underfunctioning in another. While he was involved in porn, pretending to be working (overfunctioning), he was not attending to his family relationships (underfunctioning). The reality was exposed when he tried to seduce (his point of view) or assault (her point of view, owing to the force he used) a mutual friend. The shock wave reverberated through the family.

Have you ever done too much of anything? Think about it for a moment. Many people admit to spending hours a day on Facebook, email communication, texting, or video games. One of my clients said her upset boyfriend sent her one hundred eighty-seven texts in one day.

Other things that can get out of hand or get in the way of life and relationships are gambling, porn, alcohol, illegal drugs, prescription drugs, OCD (obsessive compulsive disorder) rituals, and other self-harm behaviors such as cutting or purging.

One up/one down relationships, because they serve a purpose for the two parties, can go unrecognized just like the other anxiety-binding mechanisms. Recognizing this pattern in your relationships is the first step to seeking better ways to structure and heal these relationships, and therefore get your real needs met.

Reciprocal behaviors

In the midst of a primary style, whether going one up or one down, the person often has some area of life in which they are practicing the opposite style.

For instance, a workaholic is usually one down in their spousal and parenting relationships. The other spouse who is one up in the parenting relationships may also be avoiding the marital relationship (one down), which seems easy to do because the partner just isn't home.

A key point is that the couple in reciprocity is getting something out of the pattern or they would not tolerate it. It is binding their anxiety, and that is rewarding the pattern.

Just like the other anxiety-binding mechanisms, overfunctioning/underfunctioning reciprocity can hurt all parties involved, as we saw from Vanessa's story. Why? Because it doesn't resolve anxiety. It doesn't solve problems. Problems multiply over time through this anxiety-binding category, like all the others.

Reciprocity gradually increases anxiety. Reciprocal behaviors can feel so right and necessary for both people. But they keep the people preoccupied and distracted from their own deeper needs. Those needs are for self-respect and self-acceptance as well as mutual respect, caring, balance, and equality in the relationship or in the family.

Codependence may be more familiar than reciprocity

Codependency is a relatively new word. Once coined, it took root. It identifies something we have experienced, such as when we gave ourselves up for a relationship. More examples will follow.

Here's the story about how the word developed:

Since drug addictions and alcoholism shared more similarities than differences, beginning in the early 1980s, various drug treatment programs adopted the term chemical dependency to reflect the similarities between alcoholism (alcohol addiction) and other drug addictions.

With a unifying diagnostic term, treatment for all chemical/drug addictions coalesced into a unified treatment paradigm—chemical dependency.

To fit in with the changes, co-alcoholism (when two people in a relationship are both alcoholics) was updated to co-chemically dependent. Being too much of a mouthful, the phrase was shortened to codependent (Rosenberg, 2013).

Codependency eventually meant the person who is enabling, or shifting their own functioning significantly, to remain in relationship with a person who seems more committed to a chemical (or a negative behavior pattern) than to their relationships.

Bowen's team described the pattern in the 1950s. They saw a much broader application to the pattern than only addiction. Drug or alcohol addiction need not be the focus of the problem, but it can be included. Bowen enthusiasts sometimes use the term dysfunction in a spouse, rather than overfunctioning/underfunctioning reciprocity. The dysfunction could be physical, emotional, social, or addictive. Thus, it helps us to understand a much larger territory of human behavior than addiction alone.

To return to codependence, it need not have rigid roles, though it can. It is a basic pattern where one assumes a greater level of knowledge, skill, capability, or even integrity while the other assumes or accepts a lesser level. In codependence, two people become rather addicted to one another—relationship addiction. Or we could use Bowen's term, fused relationships.

For instance, I had a relative who had a high position in a national corporation and appeared very high functioning. It was confusing to see him with his alcoholic wife, who got embarrassingly out of control in public settings. They managed like that for more than fifty years until she passed away. (Ironically the accident that eventually took her life happened when he was drinking and driving).

Viewing it from the outside, it was very hard to understand. Bowen's point of view helped me see the two were at equal levels of emotional maturity, and only appeared to be over- and underfunctioning. Bowen would say the husband was borrowing self from his wife. In a conversation with her, I could see that she was willingly giving up self for her husband. She said she would do whatever it took to make him happy. I eventually learned from their daughter that this included wife swapping activities.

This pattern can begin subtly. It may begin for reasons based in reality, such as a temporary disability due to illness or injury, or a parent raising a child. Or it can be that a spouse is working to get the other spouse through college or a career training program that is very demanding. Both accept the temporary pattern as a necessity.

When the pattern continues beyond necessity, it can become an anxiety-binding mechanism. It becomes comfortable. In time, reciprocity will increase and become uncomfortable.

The concept of reciprocity expands the understanding of this pattern. It implies that these roles can flip, but they do not move to equality or balance without conscious, persistent effort.

Codependency in a broader sense

Though Bowen avoided focusing on a specific type of addiction, I find the word useful and rather universal if we use a looser definition that makes room for all of us to have our addictions.

It is so easy for us humans to get addicted to anything. We can be addicted to relationships. Within our relationships, we can be addicted to the one up position, and as a result seek greater position and power, greater wealth, greater advantages without ceasing. This is addiction. We are not satisfied, and seek more and more with less and less benefit. Some wealthy people are like this.

Or we can become addicted to the one down position, choosing relationships with people who are emotionally overbearing, destructive, or abusive. Or, we can become addicted to any other anxiety-binding category, such as conflict (ragaholic), distance or triangling.

The following story from a training for professional therapists exemplifies the universal nature of addiction (or if you wish, attachment).

An addictions researcher, Dr. Robert Miller, was teaching one hundred therapists his fascinating EMDR approach to addictions called the feeling-state addiction protocol (FSAP). He introduced the practicum section of the training by asking us to determine what addiction we wanted to get help with that day.

I was amused that no one raised a hand to say, "Excuse me, I don't have an addiction." Personally, I was thrilled to realize I could work on my internet email addiction.

I was equally stunned to admit to myself that I had an email addiction. I had been overfunctioning with email communication but neglecting my relationships with family members and my own spiritual life in the process. Those were my underfunctioning realms.

I became hooked on email when I met a lovely colleague online. She was so fun to communicate with by email or by phone. We had so many passions in common! It got to the point that within a few months I was spending up to four hours a night online. I couldn't stop it, even though my internet activity was not always devoted to conversations with her.

I was very grateful to Dr. Miller and my beginner colleague for practicing the EMDR FSAP protocol on me. That one practicum session helped me overcome this addiction!

This is where EMDR gives added hope to the goals inspired by Bowen theory.

Which way is up (from one up/one down)

Back to Bowen theory. In 1977 in graduate school at the University of Minnesota, I had the great opportunity as an intern to work at the Chronic Pain Treatment Program at U of M Hospital. We had a multi-disciplinary team to evaluate patients on many levels.

Physicians assessed the problem to see if any stone of current medical knowledge had been left unturned. If so, a medical solution was pursued. If the doctors concluded that no known medical solution was available, the goal was to teach the patients to live with the pain.

The team involved in this program consisted of physical therapists/personal trainers, nurses, and social workers, including myself as a social work intern.

When we are one up in one area of our lives, we are often one down in other areas. It is very hard to live a balanced life under the influence of this anxiety-binding mechanism.

We can be addicted to the one down position. I found this to be true for our chronic pain patients. Please understand I say that with great compassion and no judgment.

Our patients found it difficult, if not impossible, to express their needs. When they became injured, their signs of pain rather eloquently expressed their need. When they had a kind caregiver such as a spouse, children, or parents who jumped to help, more than ever before in their history, there was a certain joy to receiving the loving care so easily. We might say they became addicted to the care and the caregivers became unintended enablers of the pain problem.

This interaction between patient and caregiver was assessed behaviorally by the social workers, so I was vividly aware of it. As we educated patient and family, they could begin to see the pattern, too. Our job was to help the caregivers see that although their caring efforts were lovely, they were actually rewarding their loved ones' pain and increasing it.

Interestingly, another element rewarding the pain was pain medication. Most of the patients at this point were addicted to pain meds, though they were probably the people most vehemently striving not to be addicted.

They only used the meds when absolutely necessary, and the medication relieved the pain. We taught them that their body was learning through this pattern of taking meds based on pain. The body was inadvertently being trained to be in greater pain.

Sounds crazy, doesn't it? It was as if the cells had intelligence and were thinking, "If only I can amp the pain up high enough, I will finally get my reward." This is the simple principle of learning theory: whatever is followed by a positive becomes reinforced or strengthened.

We educated the patient that if they took the medication on a strict time schedule guided by the clock rather than pain, the part of their pain that had been rewarded by meds would be extinguished—removed.

The same principle applied to the caregivers. We asked the patient to give permission to the caregivers to stop responding to pain behavior such as wincing, groaning, and so on. Instead, we advised the patient to consciously choose whether they needed help, and if so, to request it verbally. This was essentially a plan to introduce more balance and equality. They agreed to it and the difficult task of changing habits began.

The eight-week program included psychotherapy to assist with the challenge of letting go of pain behavior as a way to ask for needs, and learning to ask for needs to be met in a variety of ways rather than just the needs related to pain.

The patients got better! They actually had less pain, though no physical treatment for the pain had been prescribed. The exception was physical therapy and a very gradually-increased workout program. That helped remove the pain from muscle atrophy due to not exercising muscles.

I'll never forget the twenty-five-year-old construction worker who suffered so much from his pain. He arrived walking like an unhealthy eighty-year-old-man, achingly slow, gasping with pain.

After the eight-week program, he had improved so much he looked like a healthy twenty-five-year-old construction worker. He walked upright with strength and purpose. He regained his musculature. He smiled regularly and looked energetic.

It was a wonderful experience for me to see what dramatic change could happen for what I would later see as an underfunctioning person—unhappily one down. He had the good fortune to find his way back up.

My mother eventually slid into underfunctioning regarding her arthritis. I'm grateful she was able to share the best lesson she learned about the value of diet. This helped me overcome arthritis in my thirties. However, she could not practice it herself. The sad lessons learned about one up/one down will be shared in the follow-up book.

Risks of reciprocity

As the one up person continues their overfunctioning, they tend to overdo even more over time. Isabelle was a capable, intelligent woman who previously had two full time jobs. After a number of years, she reached total exhaustion mentally and physically. Her body rebelled with chronic fatigue and fibromyalgia. She quit work and had not returned more than a decade later.

Isabelle came to me at that point because she still had so much anxiety and pain that her life was intolerable. By the time she completed her treatment, she was engaged in a passion that gave her joy, and had far less pain and emotional distress.

The risk of overfunctioning is some form of collapse. The charm of overfunctioning is that you gain a lot of perks, admiration, bonuses, etc. along the way to burnout.

One down people risk low self-esteem, and a sense of being frozen and unable to act in their highest good. The risks for behavioral addictions such as sex or gambling are loss of job, home, reputation, and support system. When chemical addiction is involved, the eventual risks are DUIs, overdoses, and even manslaughter charges.

In 2017 we witnessed this in large numbers with powerful public figures losing their jobs due to numerous allegations of sexual misbehaviors and assaults. They had been taking advantage of their one up position repeatedly. Once the #MeToo movement enabled victims to come forward and share their reality, a tide turned in the power differential. The power of the new group started to bring more equality into what had been an imbalance. It is a healthy development.

I've seen some severe risks in the overfunctioning/
underfunctioning reciprocity pattern. Figure 9.1 shows how the
pattern progresses over time. The up arrows on the left indicate
overfunctioning. The down arrows on the right indicate
underfunctioning. More arrows mean the problem is

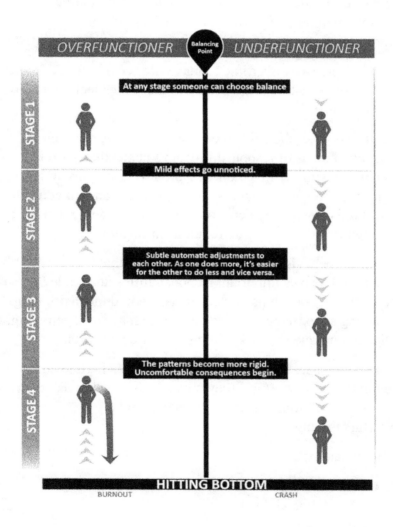

FIGURE 9.1. Risks of overfunctioning/underfunctioning

intensifying. In the end, neither party wins. Both risk hitting bottom, whether by burnout or a crash.

What to do if you are one up or one down

One up behavior can mean caregiving, being a helicopter parent who hovers over their children, being a star workaholic for the corporation and so on. Or, it can be dominating, abusing, manipulating behavior—the dark side of overfunctioning.

Some people work overtime to make life seem more desirable for themselves while other people in their lives feel the loss of their presence.

If you find yourself in the overfunctioning role, ask yourself: What other areas of responsibility am I neglecting? Am I having fun with my loved ones? Do I have a support system anymore? Overfunctioners' support systems can wither and almost die through neglect. Conversely, they can be revived by shifting priorities to nurture relationships again.

One down behavior can be a preoccupation that leaves life unbalanced, leaves important responsibilities unattended to, and leaves relationships neglected. This could mean drinking, practicing an extreme hobby or secret such as porn, gambling, collecting unique expensive items, or extreme sports.

In the latter case, the person may function at a high level in their extreme sport. But if they make decisions that risk their life rashly, omitting reasonable decision-making is underfunctioning.

Burnout can look like:

- Illness
- Mental breakdown
- Addiction
- Fleeing

Crash can look like:

- Severe addiction
- DUI or car accident
- Manslaughter, murder, or suicide
- Severe physical dysfunction
- Death

The one up/one down pattern is common to higher-functioning people. They may move into it subtly, like the frog in the water being slowly heated. The frog doesn't notice the heat in time to jump out. It can take decades for the pattern to take a noticeable toll. That is the seduction of the anxiety-binding mechanism. There are enough rewards in the beginning to keep it going.

One up often looks socially acceptable or even admirable. Modern corporations highly value a one up worker, until the worker burns out.

Reason for optimism

The good news with any anxiety-binding mechanism is this: once you are conscious of the pattern and its risks, you can offer yourself a choice:

- Can I practice the opposite maturity-building principles a little more?
- Might I use the anxiety-binding pattern a little less?

Each time you answer "Yes!" to one of these questions, you are on your way to greater freedom and emotional maturity.

Reciprocity travels through a family, with consequences

My iBE client, Georgia, struggled with incapacitating panic since early adulthood. It eventually caused a breakdown. She struggled with depression and severe chronic illnesses as well.

Her early home life had a gloom over it, as her father was a rager who often criticized her mother vehemently. But he could turn on the kids, too. Georgia felt regularly terrorized.

She arrived for her appointment one day saying she had been extremely triggered on a Sunday evening as she watched TV with her husband. The program showed a woman being abused by her husband.

Even though Georgia's husband is very supportive, the thought hit her hard: "I can't trust men." Then came the emotion: "I feel angry at men in general." She felt very bad about it, because her husband was nothing like these negative male images.

I asked her, "What is the worst image that comes up as you think about that program?"

"It was the look of fear and shock after the woman was hit by her husband."

Georgia realized quickly that this fear of men had to do with her father's rages, and her mother's constant state of trepidation as she tiptoed around her husband. Her mom "made nice" or apologized for things that weren't her doing to accommodate her husband's hypersensitive emotions.

Georgia said she and her siblings weren't safe with their father, either. If crossing a major street, he didn't think to reach for their little hands to keep them safe. Their mother had to scurry to grab all three as they crossed the street.

Having done a lot of previous iBE work, before we started the EMDR on this issue Georgia realized that her father had no protective instinct.

I asked how that could be. She said it was a result of his own father believing you should never depend on anyone. Her father had been the Lone Ranger—on his own. He raised his children the same way.

Since she was already aware that she became triggered because of the past abuse she witnessed and experienced, instead of focusing on the TV program, we focused on the historical routine: watching the very uncomfortable dance between her parents every day after Dad came home from work.

The worst image that came to mind was watching her mother in a constant state of trepidation.

When children see negativity, they identify with it in some way. I asked Georgia to explain her negative, self-limiting beliefs when she focused on the image. Her response was:

- I'm on my own.
- I can't trust men.

The positive beliefs she wanted to feel true?

- I have a supportive community of men and women.
- No one person can meet all my needs.

At the moment, the positive belief didn't feel very true to Georgia. On a seven-point scale where seven felt absolutely true at a gut level, and one felt not at all true, Georgia rated her positive belief as a two.

I asked Georgia, "As you picture that image of your Mom, and think about the negative beliefs that you are on your own and can't trust men, what emotion do you feel now?

"Deep sadness."

"Where do you feel that in your body?"

"It feels very heavy under my eyes, in my face, chest, and arms.

"How disturbing are those heavy feelings from zero to ten, where ten is the greatest disturbance possible?"

"It's a nine," she said, looking rather small and deeply sad.

We began the EMDR processing. The letters "EM" below indicate when I guided her eye movements.

Georgia (G): "I'm scared because Mom is very weak."

Dana Terrell (DT): "Go with that." EM

G: "I hear a little kid voice saying, 'Hang in there, Mommy. Don't give up, Mommy. You're strong, Mommy.'"

DT: "Notice that voice." EM

G: "Mom used me as a crutch and sought her comfort and understanding from me."

DT: "Notice how that feels inside." EM

G: "It was a horrible weight to bear. It took a toll."

DT: "Feel that weight." EM

G: "She was such a strong, beautiful Mom who believed awful things about herself. She had strength in her early twenties. But it got beaten down."

DT: "Go with that." EM

G: "She'd been consumed by motherhood and her husband's bullying. But now she has regained herself. She's gotten counseling. She has a lot more strength now. It was different for me. I didn't have a strong sense of self to come back to."

> (As Georgia was doing a lot of integrating on her own, I didn't interrupt.)

"I'm glad she is happy now. She can stand strong now. And Dad is different, better. Though they still can vibrate their edginess, it isn't as blatant. Anyway, I choose to not spend much time with them because of that. My own biology responds to them."

> (We shifted to processing some physical issues for a while, and then I brought her back to the past image of her mom in a state of trepidation.)

DT: "What do you notice now?"

G: "I feel sad in my gut, arms, and chest, but less heavy."

DT: "Go with that." EM

G: "Mom didn't know she had options. Now she knows."

DT: "See how that feels." EM

G: "It feels liberating but odd. I don't need to protect my mom anymore. I had a role and a sense of importance. She valued my helping. I could tell she felt betrayed when I stopped doing it for her. This is making sense for the first time!! I couldn't help anymore because of panic and my illnesses. And I was really angry and overdosed on this role. It was making me sick! The sad thing is that my mom turned from me to my sister as her support. That is when my sister started having problems."

Analysis

This story deals with more than one anxiety-binding mechanism. It starts with the father's overfunctioning, demanding, and bullying with a one up stance countered by the underfunctioning of the mother. Problems intensify with each generation as reciprocity is practiced across generations. Georgia had more symptoms in her lifetime than her mother and father. As she overfunctioned for her mom, her symptoms intensified.

Georgia's mother was in a clear one down position during most of Georgia's life. As she underfunctioned, she turned to her daughter calling upon Georgia to care for her (child focus, which began to shift the mother's anxiety to her daughter), turning her into an overfunctioning child. When Georgia put her own needs aside, she was underfunctioning for herself. Her needs had not been met and she didn't know how to meet them.

Sometimes it is useful to track the anxiety-binding mechanisms, because it is rare for only one to be used. Let's track the process as Georgia told it:

1. Dad comes home overfunctioning and weaving conflict (control and blame) into his choices.
2. Mom tiptoes around in the one down position, but overfunctioning to the max to try to prevent her husband's rage.
3. Triangles: The children eat in tension, afraid of Dad, and scared to see their mother so scared. They are scared to misbehave, and yet can't help it at times. Then the rage got shifted from Mom to son (usually he couldn't be as super good as the girls could). This shows the fluidity of triangles. Rather than a child focus triangle, I call it weakness focus, because the target could be anyone in the family, not just the children.
4. Once Mom is free from Dad, she turns to Georgia to become her caregiver.
5. Georgia remembered another conversation with her mother, who told her, "Never depend on men." This was a major triangling move in which the mother

placed herself and Georgia close together and her
husband and all other men in the far end of the triangle.

Georgia's adaptive information processing (AIP) system spoke
next: "It's not necessary for people to be perfect or available
all the time. I have a supportive community of men and women
now. If I'd had it when I was young, I could have gotten
through childhood much better."

This is what I appreciate about Bowen work integrated with
EMDR and the AIP. Georgia attained this neutral feeling and
positive understanding in one fifty-minute EMDR session. I
didn't have to coach her to reach it. Her brain's AIP was the
star of the show, efficiently moving toward greater health.

As you work with your own situation more thoroughly as a
result of this detailed understanding, you will be able to change
your own tendency to over- or underfunction. Just do your
best. Sometimes you will experience success. Sometimes not.
Both occasions become good learning experiences. As you
keep working to consciously change your own role, you'll gain
strength and confidence. And others in your network will
slowly begin to respond positively. Your relationships will
change in ways that will pleasantly surprise you.

Chapter 10 introduces the maturity-building principles that
serve as a refreshing antidote to one up/one down. They consist
of equality and balance.

. . . .

At a Glance: Understanding One Up/One Down Reciprocity

- In one up/one down patterns, people can play either
  role, but rarely can achieve equality.
- One responds to stress and anxiety by overdoing. This
  person risks becoming a workaholic or habitual

caregiver who experiences eventual burnout (though it may take decades).

- Anxiety and stress have the opposite effect in the underfunctioner. This person risks not reaching his or her potential and an eventual crash, such as a DUI or other crisis.
- We all need responsibility and relaxation in balance. If we specialize in one or the other, we can get into trouble eventually through the rigidity of our style.
- Overfunctioners think they know best how to handle others' responsibilities. Others deeply resent that arrogant belief. They do all they can to thwart it.
- One up/one down patterns often include a substance or behavioral addiction.
- Reciprocity and addiction remove energy and time from talents and relationships that could become more valuable sources of satisfaction.
- Reciprocity will intensify (worsen) with each generation that it is practiced.
- Awareness of the risks of the one up/one down pattern can motivate a conscious effort to let go of this pattern.
- Understanding Bowen theory and EMDR self-help methods can help people gain neutrality about their own patterns and find energy and mind power for more rewarding choices.

Practical Tips

1. Humility balanced with self-esteem is a positive practice for overcoming reciprocity. Humility means seeing oneself as neither better than nor less than others.
2. Research the one up/one down patterns you see in your family. Observe the consequences that come to people who have practiced these patterns for years.
3. If you want to change a pattern with someone, invite them to discuss how responsibilities and respect can be shared more equally. Make room for creative solutions and compromises that can work for both of you.

Equality can look different for each unique two-person relationship.

4. Sometimes making a list of silly solutions can open you both up to something that can work. Part of the creative process is to write down all solutions without judging any of them.

Chapter 10
Choosing Balance and Equality

"Better is one's own duty though imperfect than the duty of another well-performed."

The Bhagavad Gita (III:35)

"So God created man in His own image."

Genesis 1:27

"We hold these truths to be self-evident, that all men are created equal, that they are endowed by their Creator with certain unalienable Rights, that among these are Life, Liberty and the Pursuit of Happiness."

Declaration of Independence (Jefferson, 1776)

Pop Quiz

T or F I can identify three relationships in which I enjoy an equal give and take.

T or F I am annoyed by a friend who only talks and doesn't take time to listen to me.

T or F I sometimes find myself hiding my behavior from others.

T or F I get more attention for my overdoing than anything else in life.

T or F I can't stand being stressed or pressured and prefer to take it easy most of the time.

The emotionally-mature response

Bowen considered how an emotionally-mature person would handle reciprocity if a friend, family member, or coworker was trying to deal with stress by either underfunctioning or overfunctioning in a way that impacted their life (or going one up, or one down, as Jenny Brown, PhD (1999) calls it).

My Minneapolis Bowen coach said emotionally-mature people respond to one up/one down along these lines:

- I go to the person and share my concern about our relationship, which is important to me. I take responsibility for my part.
- I affirm that I value equality and balance in our relationship and in our responsibilities.
- I ask if the other person feels some need for this, too.
- If so, I ask, "How can we balance our relationship, share responsibilities in a more equal way, and practice more respect for one another?"

Creating equality

In Roberta Gilbert's book, *Extraordinary Relationships* (1992, 102-103), Dr. Gilbert writes about Bowen's observation:

> Since theoretically two people are not interested in spending time together unless they are at the same level of differentiation or emotional maturity, a basic equality of emotional maturity is present in any partnership. One might wonder, this being the case, how the overfunctioning/underfunctioning posture is able to occur.
>
> Even though levels of differentiation are equal, any partnership can have the effect of enhancing the functioning of one of the members, while compromising the functioning of the other. This results from the borrowing and lending of functional self. The partners end up with one doing better than the other, in unequal functioning postures.

Gilbert is using Bowen's term, functional self. Bowen believed individuals have a basic level of emotional maturity and a functional level. For overfunctioners, the basic level is lower than the way they want to be perceived. The way they want to be perceived is the functional level.

It's like the person who puts on a great act when meeting you for the first time, but over time you find the person isn't really like that. They can't maintain the impressive behavior consistently. Bowen thought we could not increase the basic level much at all, but even if we increase it a few points we can make a significant difference in the course of our lives.

Regarding Gilbert's discussion of equality, the way to improve this situation is simple in concept: Gilbert says, ". . . either partner, seeing self as equal to the other, can change the situation."

Gilbert goes on to explain:

> Equality is not based on tallying up individual assets; rather, it is a relationship stance, a posture assumed by the individuals. Each accepts the other as no more and no less talented, responsible, or free than him- or herself. Respect for the other, so often pointed to as essential for relationship success, is based on the equal posture. While equal partners certainly do things for each other and divide the labor or tasks of the relationship according to interests and ability, equality does not include patterned over- or underfunctioning.

I find that the sooner a one up/one down pattern is addressed, the better. The longer we travel down a particular road, the harder it is for both parties to change. And for some, it is hard to even think about change.

224 When I Do Relationships So Right How Do They Go So Wrong

Bowen learned that it is generally easier for the overfunctioner to relax their functioning a bit than for the underfunctioner to increase in functioning.

Encouragement can help a motivated underfunctioner to consciously pick up his functioning. There is no reason the encouragement can't come from within if you can't find it outside yourself. Begin with a small goal. Remember Bowen's mantra, that even microscopic progress is huge? Plan a small effort once a day or once a week. Keep at it for a month. Then review how you're doing and decide if you want to try another small goal.

This is similar to the method Ben Franklin used to improve himself. The difference is that he initially aimed for a very high ideal: perfection. I don't recommend this, and it didn't take him long to reach the same conclusion. Straining for perfection would be sliding into the risks of overfunctioning, as we saw in the diagram in chapter 9.

To keep the relationship relatively equal, clear boundaries are important. Otherwise, it can be tempting for either person to become too strong in the relationship's balance of power. Frustration and dysfunction will result. Harmony and vitality will be lost. Chapter 11 covers ways to develop clear boundaries.

Taking responsibility for self

When you sincerely take responsibility for self, it can become a rewarding process, very engaging. It comes from self-respect and grows more self-respect naturally.

Benjamin Franklin (1791) at first sought to "live without committing any fault at any time."

That negative focus quickly proved impossible to attain. He found his negative qualities seemed to multiply.

Franklin decided to positively focus on thirteen virtues he wanted to strengthen. He kept practicing one a week for thirteen weeks, and repeated the process four times a year, for years. This did work.

At age seventy-nine while writing his autobiography, Franklin concluded:

> Tho' I never arrived at the perfection I had been so ambitious of obtaining, but fell far short of it, yet I was, by the endeavour, a better and a happier man than I otherwise should have been if I had not attempted it.

He was one of the pioneers at self-improvement. A friend of his told him he was pompous and proud. So he listened receptively and added humility as the thirteenth virtue. His efforts greatly contributed to the birth of our nation. And they kept him busy.

It seems to me that self-improving people are so busy with their goals that they rarely try to pressure others to improve. Because they practice respect for others, they may request change or cooperation. Or they may give a strong hint, as Franklin's friend did. But beyond that, Franklin conducted his own self-improvement project. No one demanded that he change. He took the liberty to design and implement the project himself.

The benefit of reducing expectations of others

Bowen's other mantra, when working for change, was "set your expectations of others as close to zero as possible." With expectations, we risk becoming controlling. We want things to go our way. When they don't, we might become angry or disappointed. Thus, expectations often increase problems.

The exception is when there is a true hierarchy, such in a boss/employee relationship or teacher/student relationship. It is very important for a responsible leader to have clear expectations and set up a logical plan for helping the trainee or student achieve those expectations.

The same can be said for a responsible parent training their child in the skills that prepare their child for success in life. There is some inherent hierarchy, but the spirit of the relationship can still be full of balanced respect and equality. Both can appreciate one another for playing their role well.

My father was like this with me. I loved him for it. It taught me that sincere respect is one of the best parenting methods available. Out of his respect, he had positive (but relaxed) expectations of me.

In general, in the relationship realm, we need to be careful with expectations. If they come from anxiety, they can amp up anxiety. Notice if you react emotionally to someone's failure to do what you wanted. It is excellent feedback that you had an expectation.

Why put our set point near zero? When the other person is free from the anxiety of our desires, the slight increase in calmness often helps them take the higher road. Maybe it will take minutes, hours, or days, but I find progress comes quicker the lower you can set your expectations of others.

Let me share an example from my own life. Coming from the child-focused position, I tended to be fairly emotional (until beginning my long-term work on Bowen theory). I had high expectations of people, and when they didn't match my expectations it was an unhappy matter for them as well as me.

My Bowen coaches helped me make room for others to have their own agenda. They helped me to communicate calmly when I had a goal, maintaining maximum flexibility and patience while keeping my expectations low. Some magic would happen then. My needs were met more frequently, though not always. My relationships were far more relaxed and satisfying.

Does that mean we can set expectations of ourselves equally low? Well, it is possible. But I don't recommend it unless you are exhausted and need to let go and chill. Once you regain your energy and your dedication to growth, get clear on your purpose.

Motivated people seeking emotional maturity have the greatest power there is: the self-control to change themselves according to principles they believe in wholeheartedly. If we have clear expectations for ourselves and patiently work for them, we should experience more success—because we have control of ourselves. We do not have control of others.

Changing and letting go of one up/one down roles

When mature people discover they are in a one up/one down pattern, they take responsibility for it. Keep in mind, change starts with you changing yourself. Then the magic kingdom opens. Because you are in a system of relationships, when one person changes it sends a ripple effect through the system. If you calmly and kindly hold to a significant change, based in principle or theory, others cannot help but change if they stay connected to you and the relationship system of which you are both part.

It is not easy to let go of our ABM (anxiety-binding mechanism) roles, especially when they come naturally to us.

Martin's role has been intense overfunctioning at work to earn the acceptance of others (he called himself an overachiever). He attended the iBE Workshop and did EMDR trauma work individually on early traumas for four months.

In his last session, Martin reported, "I'm no longer bullying myself to the point of burnout. I'm now led by curiosity and tell myself, 'Let's just see what happens next.'" What I hear in this comment is that he is kindly giving himself time to assess the effect of his choices.

After learning many details about the anxiety-binding mechanisms and maturity-building principles through this book, you should be able to self-reflect and make significant changes in the way you approach any less than optimal situations in your relationships. People who are training as counselors and therapists practice using new tools in their own lives. Practice is the best way to grow your ability to use the tools effectively.

If you are ready to let go of roles that no longer serve you, like the one up or one down roles, make a list of the benefits you can expect from this effort. Keep the list in a handy place where you can see it every morning. Add to the list as you discover new benefits along the way. I think you will find that your efforts become self-rewarding.

Resolving reciprocity when it appears

Bowen shared the following story of his client's efforts to let go of old ways. It exemplifies how quickly patterns can shift. I like to think of reciprocity as an old-fashioned see saw. It can go up and down but cannot easily stay level and balanced.

Andrea was a therapist who wanted to go home to work on self. This is a common practice Bowen encouraged for anyone who wants to practice theory in their lives and gain the fruits of greater differentiation of self (emotional maturity).

"Going home" in a researcher mindset enables you to observe the patterns and your part in them. One goal while doing this is to note the sequence of anxiety-binding mechanisms, or maturity-building principles you and your relatives use naturally.

Awareness is the beginning of change. Observing the consequences of your actions is a great motivator. Observing with a fresh mindset helps you see the ways others handle their anxiety. You will find different people specialize in different anxiety-binding mechanisms. Some are more sensitive to one person's ABM than another's. Let yourself be curious about the part you play in the interactive process.

Andrea realized it wasn't very relevant for her to go home to her own mother. During the first seven years of her life, she had been raised by a Swedish nanny. So she contacted the nanny in Sweden to ask if she could visit. By now Andrea was in her mid-fifties and the former nanny, Klara, was in her seventies and single. Both were thrilled to plan a month's visit.

The two spent a joyous two weeks together reconnecting and exploring Sweden. Klara was very healthy and able to lead many activities. But one morning, she said she couldn't get out of bed. She asked Andrea to attend to her, which Andrea happily did.

As the days went by, Klara was doing less and less and becoming more and more demanding. It dawned on Andrea that she was playing a role in this problem by over-doing. So, she deliberately started to underfunction. When Klara asked for tea in the kitchen cupboard (and described the location to a "T") Andrea told her, "Gee, I'm having the hardest time finding it."

Klara insisted the tea was in that exact location. She was right. This was quite a trial for both of them. Bowen may or may not have endorsed what the therapist, Andrea, chose to do. But his chief goal was for people to think about the theory and make decisions with theory in mind. He didn't give techniques or rules.

Andrea made her changes thoughtfully, based on theory, while she metaphorically shook in her boots. Klara's frustration fueled more intense criticism, vocal power, and almost disgust. This was painful after the wonderful harmony they had shared.

But finally, after many hours, Klara said, "Well, I'll just have to get up and get it myself!" Which she did, without any major problem.

The former nanny began to do more and more for herself, and her short-term decline was fully over by the time the therapist headed back to the US. Andrea did not abandon her kindness and joy in being with Klara, so the relationship managed to bounce back from the difficulty.

Ways to approach your request for equality

It's common with Bowen theory for people to change their behavior rather than telegraph their changes and reasoning. The approach is up to the individual. My way is more open and collaborative. I am uncomfortable pretending or posturing.

So, if you have a need for the other to change, I believe it is OK to request that change. But again, it's best to have zero expectations. Otherwise the anxiety of your wishes will interfere with their ability to decide for themselves with their self-respect intact.

An exception to this guidance would be if you have a non-negotiable "I" position. "I" positions will be addressed further in chapter 11.

The most emotionally-mature people Bowen knew were uncomfortable about getting stuck in either role, whether it was called overfunctioning/underfunctioning reciprocity, as Bowen called it, or one up/one down as Jenny Brown, PhD refers to it.

If they found themselves in such a pattern, they said they would often bring it up to the other person. It might be their spouse, their child, a friend, a coworker, or their mother.

If one was slacking off in their responsibilities and the other was taking on more than their share, it was addressed descriptively. They said things like, "I can see I'm letting things slide and you have been taking up the slack. I appreciate it but it's not fair to you. Can we look at ways to share our responsibilities more fairly?"

Of course, this is a pretty easy conversation, because you are not asking more of your loved one. And, yes, it is easier for the overfunctioner to let go of overfunctioning than for the underfunctioner to pick up their mode. But nothing is impossible. Any motivated person can begin to make slow, steady, regular efforts and they will gain the benefit.

If the one down person would like the one up person to change, they can let them know they need them to back off a little. When I was a college student, my generous father got in the habit of sending $500 to me with random timing. After I graduated, he continued. I became dependent upon it, but the problem was that I couldn't rely on it. I helplessly waited for it to arrive.

Frustrated, I realized this was interfering with my ability to be an independent adult. I was ready to become an equal. I talked with Dad about it like this:

> Thank you, Dad for all the support you've given me over the years. At this point it is actually causing a problem for me. It is making it hard for me to trust my ability to support myself. So I ask that you not send monetary gifts unless it is Christmas or my birthday.

He quietly agreed to my request, honored it in practice, and never mentioned it again.

There may be specific challenges when working with a partner. Perhaps you are overfunctioning and you want to invite the other to chip in more equitably. The other person may be sensitive. Self-esteem suffers in the one down position.

Describing your awareness and inviting a creative way to make it more balanced can work in this situation. I find it helpful to be brief with sensitive people and emphasize the positive request rather than giving negative feedback. One example is to say, "I have a request for a little more equality in our relationship." It gets the person focused on what you want. There is no need to defend.

When a caregiver asks for help

There are times when reality calls for caregivers and a care receiver. Someone is ill, or injured, or vulnerable in some way. Perhaps it is a terminal illness. Or it could be a chronic illness such as arthritis, fibromyalgia, heart disease, diabetes, COPD, or chronic fatigue. Perhaps an injury or trauma leads to pain and weakness. There is a recovery process, and the outcome may or may not be what was desired and hoped for.

Or perhaps one person has lost a very important relationship, or job, or had to move from a cherished place. Or they may have lost their sense of safety or control due to an experience of abuse, whether at the workplace, in a relationship, or random crime.

My parents were proud they had raised four children who get along effectively and happily as adults. And they personally benefitted from our team spirit when they were struggling in the declines of old age.

Dad let us know he was overwhelmed by the caregiving role. Our parents had thought with all the friends they had retired with, they would have a large support system. But after Mom's amputation, in her depression she would not allow friends to visit. Dad sadly told us that he was on his own. He wanted to move closer to us, but mom resisted the idea.

We came for a family meeting to discuss things and lay out options. At the time, we proposed to Mom that since she was not receiving the help of friends we hoped she would accept the help of family members in California. We affirmed both of them needed more support. Mom was hesitant, but we all assured her we would do what we could to make the transition as comfortable and smooth as possible. So she agreed.

Mom and Dad moved to the area of California where they would have two of their children nearby, for the most significant support. I was further away and offered to come as needed.

This situation worked very well for our family, with everyone feeling considered, comfortable, and supported. This solution worked for eight years.

Other ways to prevent caregiver burnout

To prevent the caregiver from burnout, it is good to cultivate a support system through an online community such as Lotsa Helping Hands or Caring Bridge as my husband David and I did when he was diagnosed with cancer. The concepts used by these websites save a lot of communication effort. Friends who want to help can be given access to post notices or requests for specific kinds of assistance.

As days turned into months during my husband's illness, I wanted to offer my strengths without stealing his. He was willing to have me do the research I wanted to do to find solutions. He had no interest in doing that, but was willing to listen to what I had learned. He always maintained control over the choices.

When he made a choice, he embraced it with great focus and discipline. And the results showed it. He lived five times longer than the doctor expected.

Fortunately, after the diagnosis, because of some of the solutions he used he no longer had pain.

Learning and unlearning one up/one down

For those who have pain, there is a challenge for the caregiver and receiver. Chapter 9 covers my intern work at the U of M Chronic Pain Treatment Program. We taught relatives and patients there is no drawback to offering great loving care for three weeks. But beyond that point, attentive care from the caregiver as well as pain medication can actually reward the patient's pain and increase it. The body can learn to produce pain to receive the benefit.

Our treatment program taught patients and family to make caregiving behaviors and delivery of pain meds independent of pain perceptions and pain behaviors such as grimaces, groans, and so on. This was successful in helping to reduce the pain.

There is another danger. The learning process also rewards codependent (one up/one down) patterns. Yet several of my caregiver clients who found themselves overfunctioning have commented: "The more I gave, the more they took." This awareness helped them begin to let go of overdoing the caregiver role.

To solve this problem, at the pain program we taught patients to become more conscious of their ability to meet their own needs or to ask directly when they couldn't meet their own needs (rather than relying on pain behaviors such as moaning or wincing). Thus, they were taking on more responsibility as they were able, and the caregiver had less responsibility.

When a relationship has one up/one down aspects, the goal becomes to have optimum health maintained as much as possible, whenever possible. My friend Rose had a surgery, and commented, "It is easy to focus on the pain and discomfort, but I remind myself that all my other parts are working well. It helps me balance my attitude."

Being conscious as a care receiver

Whatever it is that necessitates playing a care receiver role, look for ways to fulfill your potential. It is easy to think less of yourself when you cannot do what you did before. But you still have plenty of strengths, and perhaps some opportunities you didn't have before. Focus on your strengths and watch for new strengths to arise.

My husband went on disability about five months after his stage IV cancer diagnosis. He was having trouble with the physical responsibilities of his job. David's additional strengths included music and his spiritual life. He began to fill his days with the joy of these pursuits, as well as doing as much as he could around the house to help me. His spiritual activities helped him feel more love, he told me, for everyone and everything. He didn't expect that to happen.

So watch for new strengths to arise in you. Get curious about what they will be.

Social patterns of one up/one down

To see beyond the personal to the societal level, for moving beyond the one up/one down pattern, we have great examples. Several leaders successfully guided their people from their one down position to overcome the one up position of the ruling class of white Europeans or white Americans.

Elizabeth Cady Stanton and Susan B. Anthony laid the foundation for women to gain the vote from the men who initially laughed at the notion as preposterous. They pooled their intelligence, determination, and vision to guide and energize a movement that continued beyond their lives.

Susan B. Anthony was a genius for spreading the word and took the mission on the road. Elizabeth Cady Stanton maintained her roles as wife and mother but invigorated the movement with her wisdom and wit.

Mahatma Gandhi, Martin Luther King, and Nelson Mandela all exhibited the strengths of emotionally-mature people. They did what they knew to be right. When they made a mistake, they often admitted it and did their best to overcome the pattern. None were perfect beings. But, the strength of and commitment to their deepest principles brought a successful transfer of power that was as peaceful as possible.

Other leaders whose maturity have influenced our nation and the world are American natives. We learned many precepts of American democracy from the Iroquois.

Unfortunately, the equality between the sexes enjoyed by the Iroquois was ignored by the long-standing patriarchal one up tradition. The men in power couldn't comprehend such a way of life. It didn't even enter discussion, though the issue of slavery was heatedly discussed as our nation was laboring to be born.

The northern founding fathers who passionately wanted a nation free of slavery surrendered to the southern founders, who would have refused to join the country if slavery was outlawed. So, though Americans affirmed our ideal of equality for all men, it did not originally extend to all.

As Lincoln wrote in 1858, "As I would not be a slave, so I would not be a master. This expresses my idea of democracy. Whatever differs from this, to the extent of the difference, is no democracy."

Lincoln helped us work toward a more perfect union, as did Stanton and Anthony. It is a continuing labor, a continuing birthing process. The old ways of holding on to ideas of supremacy, of one up, are intoxicating to those addicted to them. So, too are the experience of real equality and balance. I would say that the latter offer a higher high. But if you only have experience living with one way, you may be certain of that way—not so certain of the new way.

Just as balance is an ongoing practice throughout our lives, so is equality. The status is never fixed or rigid. Each relationship goes through adjustments, some mini and some mega as needs and interests change.

Our culture will continue to adjust to our ideals, and struggle for that more perfect union. If we keep balance and equality alive in ourselves and in our relationships and our culture, we will keep both our self-respect and our respect for our fellow being intact. We will have a healthy balance of the principle essential for individual health—a strong sense of self, and the essential principle for societal health—a sincere, caring interest in the well-being of the whole.

Balance and equality are possible for all people

I've given some famous examples of balance and equality. But this state is well within the reach of more ordinary mortals. Remember Beth in chapter 3 on conflict? She watched her future father-in-law suddenly choke her fiancé. Beth then erupted in violence for the first and only time in her life.

To see Beth's most recent success story, just two weeks after her iBE Workshop and two months after the violence incident, visit ibetherapy.com/relationshipresources.

Shining examples of balance and equality

We just learned one great example of the equal view provided by Beth. Would you like to watch and study people who made a lifetime commitment to balance and equality for the sake of themselves and others? There are excellent films to choose from. A few suggestions:

- *Not for Ourselves Alone: The Story of Elizabeth Cady Stanton and Susan B. Anthony*, a PBS special
- *Gandhi*
- *Selma*, about Dr. Martin Luther King
- *The Long Walk to Freedom*, about Nelson Mandela's life journey

Each leader is a shining example of emotional maturity, a subject which will be further developed in my follow-up book. And yet, they are not perfect. No one is perfectly emotionally-mature, whether it is Bowen, Franklin, you, or me. But we can keep working toward the goal, and in the process, gain strength, flexibility, and all the benefits maturity-building principles offer.

If you watch these movies, note which of the maturity-building principles the main characters practice.

Chapter 11 discusses taking "I" positions. This means expressing your clear purpose, sometimes in terms of boundaries. You may find it valuable to list the "I" positions these leaders took.

Balance is dynamic
Please keep this is mind: Balance is not static, it is alive. It requires ongoing effort to strive for balance in your self-care routines and in your relationships. If you are off-balance, your heart, mind, and body will let you know. Those who care about you may also let you know. Listen with your heart.

You have now learned the four maturity-building principles:

- Understanding and empathy
- Connection and patience
- Direct commitment
- Balance and equality

Practicing these in small steps with growing consistency creates a fertile soil for the natural growth of emotional maturity. Chapter 11, Creating "I" Positions, provides a thorough step-by-step guide to a skill for growing your own maturity throughout life. This effort will reinforce all the other maturity-building principles you are gathering into your repertoire of possibilities.

. . . .

At a Glance: Choosing Balance and Equality

- Any relationship, even if relatively balanced and equal, can experience one up/one down aspects.
- Underfunctioners can increase in functioning through encouragement and taking on small goals.
- Underfunctioners can approach overfunctioners to relax their position and back off using simple, direct reasoning.
- Clear boundaries are an important aspect of balanced, equal relationships.
- It is wise to set your expectations of family members and others as close to zero as possible. This is because expectations tend to lead to control and demand behaviors, which will only increase problems.
- The exception to this is that sometimes you will need to set clear boundaries. Chapter 11 on "I" positions includes more on this subject.
- When you must be a caregiver, make sure you take sufficient time to care for yourself. This is essential if you want to avoid becoming a patient yourself.
- When you are a care receiver, look for ways to fulfill your potential. It is easy to think less of yourself when you cannot do what you did before. Focus on your strengths and watch for new strengths to arise.
- Balance is not static, it is alive. It requires ongoing effort to create. Work for balance in your self-care

routines and in your relationships. You will find it is
well worth the effort.

Practical Tips

1. If you are in a one down position, research yourself to
   discover your strengths and your dreams. Ask friends
   and family members which strengths they see in you.
   Do they remember strengths you had in the past?
   Passions or goals?
2. If you are in a one up position, research to discover the
   strengths of those closest to you. If you are having a
   hard time, interview others to learn from them.

Chapter 11
Creating "I" Positions

"When his peers applied group pressure to follow their vision, he responded: "I will do what I believe is right.""

Mandela (1994)

"I know that the core of you is the same as the core of me."

Oprah Winfrey (2018)

"As I would not be a slave, so I would not be a master. This expresses my idea of democracy."

Lincoln (1858)

Pop Quiz
T or F I have noticed that I act differently depending upon who I am with.

T or F I can think of three things I respect about myself.

T or F Even when stressed, I can maintain calm and balance in my life.

T or F I can't let it go when I run into roadblocks in my life.

T or F My decisions take into account my feelings and thoughts but are not determined by my emotions.

Definition of the "I" position
An "I" position is the ability to take a thoughtful stand, whether other people who are important to you agree or not. Taking "I" positions includes the skills and strengths to set clearly defined, calm, and consistent boundaries.

After years of practice, I enthusiastically love taking "I" positions. They give me the opportunity to let myself explore my take on something deeply, to learn what is most true for me. Bringing my behavior in sync with my values and convictions helps to grow inner strength and integrity.

That being said, it is more accurate to say that I often love the strength of "I" positions after they've been spoken. At the beginning and even now, it is sometimes awkward, anxious, and foreign to take an "I" position. I can approach the opportunity with trepidation, and occasionally bail out prematurely.

Taking an "I" position can feel wrong because it is a departure from what is familiar. It is natural to worry: "My message may not be received well. I may be rejected." It is a true risk. We often will experience initial rejection from others when we make a significant change.

When creating "I" positions, there are three steps to take.

1. Develop your "I" position.
2. Gain comfort with your position. Do a practice run and breathe through it.
3. Share your position. Then become curious. Let others have their own response while you seek to understand them and invite them to understand your position more fully.

How to develop your "I" positions

"I" positions begin with a degree of deep introspection about a situation. These questions may help you develop your position:

1. What are the facts I know about this issue?
2. Are there others who know more than I? Can I talk to them or read their books?
3. As the facts become clear, notice: Am I getting a little calmer? Bowen says facts are calming.

4. Then ask: Are my feelings becoming clear? What are they? One of my friends, highly skilled at nonviolent communication, likes to think of as many feelings as she can. It is a way for her to give herself empathy. Feelings provide useful feedback—especially if they are somewhat calm. You can calm your feelings simply by breathing into them.

5. What do I really want or need, ideally? Marshall Rosenberg's book, *Nonviolent Communication,* has a lovely section on needs. This, too, is a way to affirm yourself, and value yourself. It is nice to acknowledge a need honestly to yourself.

6. What opinions, beliefs, and values now come into play for me?

7. What do you want from the person you are speaking to? According to Rosenberg, it is most successful to express this as a request. If we make a demand, we are moving into conflict and control, or overfunctioning. Requests keep us in equality, respecting the independent choices of both parties.

8. Write down the key points you want to make when communicating your "I" position.

9. Be open to negotiation. Perhaps your listener cannot or will not do what you request, but could respond in some other supportive way.

10. After you complete the conversation, reflect on it. Ask, "How can I be true to myself and true to my relationships? What am I willing I do now?

How to be comfortable with the "I" position

I find that most of the anxiety in using an "I" position is due to not having reasoned the situation thoroughly enough, or empathized with my needs and feelings enough, or introspected, or prayed enough to come up with an "I" position that really fits for me. Thus, the above steps should be helpful.

Once I have completed these steps, it is often satisfying to share my "I" position.

This is the irony of departing from anxiety-binding mechanisms. If we practice ABMs (anxiety-binding mechanisms) we feel comfortable and righteous immediately. Only with a little time do we begin to get anxious, and with a more time and thought, begin to have regrets.

When practicing instead, a calmly-conceived "I" position, some people feel anxious right off the bat. They are making a significant change—going into the unknown. With practice and deep breathing, this will ease.

I normalize this process for my clients and group participants, meaning I let them know their feelings are normal and even predictable. If you believe you are truly wrong afterwards, of course you can amend your "I" position. But if not, I recommend continuing to breathe and allowing the process to unfold.

Allow others to have their own response

As the other person responds to your "I" position, this is a good time to be curious about their thoughts and emotions. Invite them to share more. Only they know the whole picture they must consider for their response. Listen calmly for as long as you can. Aim to listen for at least ten minutes. Listening is one of the greatest gifts you can give.

See if you can see your loved one or friend begin to relax. Then ask: "Are you feeling understood?" If the answer is "Yes," then, "Do you think you are ready to listen more to my view and feelings about this?"

Eventually you gain strength. The relationship gains clarity, calmness, and the comfort of being able to address emotional realities together. You and your relationship become more reality-based.

Bowen observed that emotionally-mature people wanted to communicate their "I" positions one-to-one with each relevant person.

This tends to prevent misunderstandings (Though it won't guarantee it!). Each person can ask questions and clear up any confusions they have. It takes time, but you are laying a foundation for future health. It is worth it.

How "I" positions help parents—and their children

"I" positions are a valuable way for parents to teach rules and principles for living. They are most effective when uttered calmly and matter-of-factly, as if you are saying that the sun comes up in the east.

Despite the fact my parents didn't hear about Murray Bowen until I was thirty-years-old, they had a natural ability to take a clear, clean, calm stand. However, there were certain times it would have helped them to be conscious of all Bowen learned about "I" positions. This was true when they faced a challenge they had never faced before.

Following are three examples of their "I" positions, plus two more by others for good measure:

I expect you to eat at least a little of the food that I cook, Therefore, I want you to take two bites of everything on the plate.

> This resulted in a family with no picky eaters. Though sometimes the person having a hard time eating their two bites had to sit alone at the table until the bites were eaten.

Being cruel to your sister/brother is unacceptable. Do I need to get the paint paddle?

"Oh, no!" we'd reply.

My parents believed in a light and quick form of corporal punishment. They used the wooden stick received from paint stores for stirring a gallon of paint. My parents called it the paint paddle. They gave us two light stings on the bare butt. It stung like crazy but faded fast.

My parents trusted this method and never became angry or out of control. We accepted it because it was tolerable, we knew we deserved it, it would be over quickly, and we knew how to avoid it in the future. Thus, we experienced very few spankings.

After age seven we were never spanked. I read in a good parenting book years later that this is a wise boundary for ending spankings. It becomes humiliating after that age. The humiliation interferes with the training goal. Instead of children learning what you want them to learn, their trust in you and in themselves will be shaken.

You are welcome to your weekly allowance when your chores have been completed each day.

We did our chores and became very good at it when quality control measures were followed.

From my sister-in-law, Laura: "You don't have to like the food, but out of respect for the cook, please thank the cook for the lovely meal."

This produced sons who know how to appreciate anyone's contribution to the meal.

Nephew Evan to his daughter: "You can either treat your cousin like a good friend or you can come sit with me."

She was too upset to be nice then, so she chose to sit with her dad. About five or ten minutes later she was ready to cooperate again.

To our son when he misbehaved at school: "Since your behavior has taken energy from the family, we need you to do a project that puts energy back in. There is a garden section that needs digging and fertilizing."

Result: He took a break every hour from the digging and came in to give me a hug. I was surprised. I believe he felt good that he could regain a position of respect.

"I" positions can be called boundaries

As you will see from the following example of Martin (a client), sometimes you can intuitively seize a good idea and run with it.

Martin is a manager who has been anxiously dealing with his boss, "Rocky," for a couple of years. Rocky finds ways to abuse Martin and his entire staff.

The abuse feels like a super chilly, cold, silent vibe. It is as if Rocky is behind a wall but loves to show people how he can poke them without recourse. Despite frequent employee complaints to human resources, Rocky has thus far been protected by the leadership of the corporation.

Martin has had many nightmares since he went from being Rocky's favorite to just another target. A thirty-minute meeting with Rocky became like an invitation to sweat bullets. It takes major effort for Martin to manage his anxiety.

At a recent session, Martin and I worked on the skill of "I" positions and boundary setting. He connected these skills with a Dutch saying he learned to enjoy while living in the Netherlands: "Strong in my shoes."

Martin reported that since that session, he embraced a question to ask throughout each day: "What are my boundaries in this situation?"

Boundaries help Martin to be strong in his shoes. If he feels any apprehension, he often visualizes a force field around himself. As he drew his visual affirmation for me, it was a generous force field, about an arms-reach around, above, and below his body.

Martin recently inherited a difficult employee from another department. The employee, Karlie, was a senior staffer who nonetheless had concerns about being disrespected. She complained about her workspace not being larger than the others. Karlie hinted at other special treatment she deserved.

Since Martin was a natural people-pleaser, in initial conversations with Karlie he reacted by trying to make her happy. He was not used to employees being aggressive about what they felt they deserved.

Martin soon wised up due to the daily mantras running through his head: "What would I perceive if I was a more socially savvy, observant, and thoughtful person? What are my boundaries in this situation? What would I expect to be reasonable if the roles were reversed?" Martin imagined the force field boundaries between himself and Karlie as being exactly halfway between the two. Not overbearing on him, not overbearing on her.

A few weeks later in the staff meeting, Karlie said in front of everybody, "Hey I want to know when someone is going to bring the snacks and drinks *I* like. I need Diet Coke!"

Martin went to his self-training, thinking about what would be reasonable if he was the employee asking. Instead of saying, "Yes of course we'll get that for you!" he said, "Just like all the other team members, you're free to purchase the snacks you need on your corporate credit card. If you're the one doing the shopping you'll be sure to get what you like." This left it to Karlie to be more self-reliant and let her know that she was subject to the same norms as everyone else. Martin explained:

> In the past, my boundaries were so minimal I was shrink-wrapped. I felt such a mission to help everyone that I let them all come in way too close. And, as a manager with the bully, I was the one in front, taking the hits for everyone else who was hiding behind me. Sometimes I, too, could be overbearing. Now by using boundaries in more situations, I'm more co-equal. It's very empowering.

Martin is drilling on his new boundaries skill like a disciplined athlete. His introspective questions enable him to be more centered and successful.

. . . .

Mother Teresa's purpose from childhood was to serve the poor. She traveled to India to pursue that vocation. Instead, she found herself in a cloistered convent, held within the convent walls.

She yearned to go out to respond to the needs of suffering people she saw through the upper floor windows. This brought her anguish.

She asked permission from her superiors to go serve them. Such exceptions always required the approval of the Pope, and much prayer and patient waiting on then Sister Teresa's part.

Because Mother General of the convent of Loreto did not share her goals, Sister Teresa in time found it necessary to petition for secularization, which essentially meant a complete separation, never to be bridged again.

She had to give up everything before she knew if she would be allowed to start a new congregation of nuns called the Missionaries of Charity. This showed the strength of her purpose. She was convinced she was doing the will of God. Thus, He would bless the purpose with success.

Her "I" position, and that which she adopted for her community, was borrowed from St. Francis in the form of a prayer:

> Lord, make me an instrument of your peace:
> where there is hatred, let me sow love;
> where there is injury, pardon;
> where there is doubt, faith;
> where there is despair, hope;
> where there is darkness, light;
> where there is sadness, joy.

Risks, costs, and opportunities of the "I" position

Anyone taking a strong "I" position may also face, to some degree, the same risks of exclusion and separation experienced by Mother Teresa.

Bowen learned that if we continue to hold to our position, communicating it clearly and consistently to relevant persons as needed, eventually the sincerity of our purpose is understood by more and more people. The initial rejection that greeted us eventually turns to respect (for many, if not for all).

Rejecting new positions, ideas, and courses of action seems to be a natural human phenomenon. We like what is known and comfortable. Many get anxious about what is unknown and new.

One of my Bowen coaches told me to be curious about who is first to understand, accept, and respect a well-conceived "I" position. That person will generally be the most emotionally-mature person in the family or group. Or, it may be the person coping with the least stress at the time.

It took Mother Teresa years to be accepted and respected by the Pope and the Catholic hierarchy. But she continued in her purpose to the best of her ability, whether she had the acceptance and full support or not.

This is often a cost of the sincere "I" position. It is also an opportunity to review and introspect: "Is this really what I believe?"

Honestly, I have begun to see rejection as a sign I may be doing something significant—making a real and beneficial change. In this case I reinterpret the pushback as a compliment.

Another possibility is that I am off base. Being open to the feedback of wise dear ones is a protection against deluding ourselves. Listen to the feedback you receive and ask yourself, "Is it true?" If it is, adjust your course. If it is not, hold to your course.

If we continue our same patterns and goals, we will find that people continue in their plodding patterns of life, giving us little notice. It sometimes takes an "I" position to wake people up, even slightly.

If we have put a lot of thought and effort into creating our own clarity, remember, others may not have devoted a similar effort. They may, in time, mentally and emotionally digest your position. Being less motivated about your "I" position, they will often do so at a snail's pace and rarely that of a jackrabbit.

"I" positions of Nelson Mandela

Nelson Mandela (1994, 2013) proceeded patiently but surely toward his purpose.

The former South African State President de Klerk set his intention (his "I" position) on being the last president of the racist country. He asked some of his ministers and other trusted officials to meet secretly with Nelson Mandela to plan his release from prison after almost thirty years. He also wanted the group to plan for a peaceful transition to power sharing.

Mandela's friends found out about the meetings and voted to tell Mandela to stop the discussion. He acknowledged their vote but told them he would do what he believed was right.

He continued the discussions. The five-person team faced emotional reality together. The head of the prisons knew that in his heart, Mandela had to want revenge for the abuse he and his family had been subjected to. Mandela agreed that he was right.

Another leader then wanted to know how Mandela expected, under that circumstance, for the whites to ever give the Africans any real power.

Mandela clarified that although he had an urge for revenge, in truth he wanted something much more. His goal was to "live without fear and hatred."

His listeners thought that was a dream beyond possibility.

Mandela then shared what he had noticed from years of oppression. He had seen the destructive power of whites full of fear, leading to brutality and injustice. He basically shared the idea that if the Africans lead in the same way, they would be sentencing themselves, their children, and future generations to a prison of the same kind of ugliness. That would leave everyone still locked up in misery. Mandela assured the team that he wanted something much better than revenge.

The ongoing calm conversation enabled Mandela to speak this strong truth. More importantly, the team listened peacefully.

They did not argue. They understood. It took a lot of mutual understanding to help a nation overcome such pain together.

Mandela took one strong position after another. He accepted his role as leader, who sometimes had to tell his people what they did not want to hear. He needed them to hear the truth. This is the process of mature, consistent leadership that brings benefit not just to one generation, but many.

In truth, it has been a painfully difficult adjustment. But without Mandela's calm, mature leadership, I believe it would have been far worse.

The need for mature leadership has never been greater

With the challenges facing America and the world in this millennium of terrorism, huge population growth drives poverty and immigration; wars cause refugees to go on the move; climate change creates an increasing pace and intensity of natural disasters.

The need for mature, farsighted leadership has never been greater. This is one of the concerns that urgently drove me to write this book while moving through the struggles of cancer and caregiving our family faced at home.

Throughout the world, as a human family, we are now concerned about these vast forces affecting us.

One man is particularly well-poised to offer wisdom and perspective. Timothy Snyder is currently Professor of History at Yale. He spent decades in Europe studying the fall of democracies in Europe in the twentieth century. Two democracies turned into fascist Italy and Nazi Germany. These countries plus the Soviet Union became tyrannies.

Now that Snyder is back in America, he is observing up close our American vulnerability to fascism. From his thorough study, similar to Bowen's scientific observer mindset, he gained a deep understanding.

One weekend after the 2016 presidential election, Snyder spontaneously wrote a small book, "about the size of the Constitution and almost as important." It's called, *On Tyranny: Twenty Lessons from the Twentieth Century.*

Snyder's chapter 12 discusses the importance of connection in day-to-day life. He encourages the simple niceties of life: to make small talk and look people in the eye. Snyder studied memoirs of victims of tyrannical regimes. He found they all reached a point where little actions between neighbors took on greater importance.

In general, Snyder's book is a succinct series of "I" positions taken by someone who has thought deeply about the patterns that make tyranny possible, and the patterns that can prevent the loss of democracy. If you hope to strengthen the democracy for the generations to come, I recommend his little gem.

When we are motivated to help the coming generations, it is most helpful to focus on playing your own part well. If we slip into any kind of an anxious focus on the future generations, our efforts will backfire. It is most powerful, and most achievable, to focus on ourselves, to choose our "I" positions with care and hold to them firmly while always remaining open to listen and learn.

Whether you seek improved relationships at home, at work, in the neighborhood, in civic life, or in national life, developing the skill of taking clear, calm "I" positions with each individual relevant to your concern is an essential practice.

Self-respect and trusting your judgment are natural outgrowths of knowing the principles you love and practicing them in daily life. Just be willing to do your best and let the chips fall where they may. You cannot control the other person's response, but you can control the calm clarity and consistent thoughtfulness of your "I" position.

I invite you to commit to the principles of Bowen theory integrated with the desensitization gained through EMDR. You could commit for a week, a month, or a lifetime. How much do you want to activate your AIP's inner strength and confidence? And how much do you want to share with others? Remember, even microscopic progress is huge.

We are at a vulnerable point in history with emotional immaturity permeating the decision-making of people at all levels of world society, from the homeless to our leaders. This causes increasing stress and trauma. This presents a great urgency as well as a great opportunity.

My hope and prayer is that we seize the opportunity do our personal best to practice the maturity-building principles we love: understanding and empathy, connection and love, direct commitment, and balance and equality. Thus, may we brighten the light shining from our lives.

As we breathe with patience, may we see that light radiating into our loved ones and beyond, planting shining seeds of maturity for the generations to come.

. . . .

At a Glance: Creating "I" positions

- An "I" position is the ability to take a thoughtful stand, whether other people important to you agree or not. It includes the skills and strengths to set clearly defined, calm, and consistent boundaries.
- Be prepared that you may receive rejection for your boundaries or "I" positions.
    - o Common messages of rejection:
        - ▪ You're wrong
        - ▪ Change back

- Or there will be consequences!
- Be as consistent in your position, and in your practice of maturity-building principles as possible.
- In time, with such a consistent and patient effort, rejection will often turn to respect. This happens sooner with more emotionally-mature people.
- The timing of acceptance may be based on the emotional maturity level, and/or the stress level of each person doing the rejecting.

Practical Tips

1. To create an "I" position and share it:
   o Ask: "What are the facts? How do I feel? What is my opinion? What are my values and beliefs? How can I be true to myself and my relationships?"
   o Plan your communication: Bowen recommended talking one-to-one with each relevant person so all are informed.
   o Facts are calming. Share facts first.
   o Invite the response of the other person. Listen.
   o Create a clear request. Do you want the other person to take action, or understand your position?
   o If the other person declines your request, accept their choice. Give others the freedom to make their own choices. They are aware of the whole picture they must consider when choosing their response.
   o Have a plan B, an alternate way to meet your need.
   o If you have an ample support system, you will often find another person who is willing to respond positively to your request.
2. To help you strengthen your new skill of taking "I" positions, keep a record of your past stands. This can help you remember past successes. You may want to

track how long it takes various people to understand
your position. When are they able to respect it?

Epilogue
Your Transformed Relationships and Beyond

"If there is righteousness in the heart, there will be beauty in
the character.
If there is beauty in the character, there will be harmony in the
home.
If there is harmony in the home, there will be order in the
nations.
When there is order in the nations, there will peace in the
world."

Confucius

The transformation of individual human relationships that
ultimately leads to world peace begins in each person's heart.
EMDR is a holistic heart, mind, body, and spirit approach you
can practice for yourself in the self-help manner described in
this book.

Shapiro contributed a brilliant gift to humankind by developing
EMDR and observing its ability to jump-start the inherent,
emotionally-mature AIP (adaptive information processing)
system. EMDR's desensitization methods enable the AIP to
unfold. The AIP is to me the source of resilience, inner
strength, wisdom—all that makes life worthwhile.

Use the power of desensitization each day of your life. When
you want to be fully present, practice the container exercise
and The Four Elements Exercise. These are valuable to
practice before doing anything important. This may mean
giving your very best effort to a project you are passionate
about, or being vulnerable and listening to an upset person you
care about, or taking an "I" position.

Bowen's uniquely valuable contribution to humankind was to bring order to the emotions and the complexity of human behavior. He revealed the necessity of emotional maturity and taught us how to access it by rooting out and replacing our hidden habits and patterns. Bowen theory guides us to cultivate our own emotional maturity by taking a stand using clear "I" positions.

The brilliance of Bowen's lasting contribution is based on his observation of the four anxiety-binding categories that encompass all problem behaviors. He clarified that ABMs (anxiety-binding mechanisms) originate from anxiety, continue to circulate, and gradually increase anxiety.

One type of ABM tends to cause others to react with another ABM, resulting in a chain reaction of increasing difficulties. Though immediately comfortable to the person who is practicing their favorite ABM (whether in a family, a circle of friends, a workplace or beyond), the health of the relationship system gradually suffers from that point on: a process of regression.

There is one potent exception to this process. When differentiated, emotionally-mature people maintain a commitment to practice balanced, healthy principles, the well-being of the system gradually increases. Consciously-practiced health, maturity, and an engaged AIP together can heal the chronic anxiety that fuels ABMs. Practicing similar principles is how noble leaders like Gandhi, Mother Teresa, and Martin Luther King grew the strength to inspire and lead others to follow high and noble principles.

What this means for you

By reading this book, you have learned the antidotes to the anxiety-binding behaviors. As you observe your own behaviors like a neutral researcher, you will see when you are prone to using a once-hidden ABM. You understand now there is no real need, or lasting benefit, for living in the anxiety-binding mode. You will be able to practice replacing all your ABMs with maturity-building principles that will heal your relationships and change your life.

Benjamin Franklin worked on overcoming one weakness at a time. Learning theory shows that at least three weeks' effort can strengthen a new habit. To overcome a tendency toward an ABM, review the corresponding maturity-building principles found in chapters 4, 6, 8, or 10, and chapter 11.

The principles are: understanding and empathy; connection and patience; direct, personal, committed relationships; and balance and equality. Additionally, Bowen recommended these key guidelines:

a. Practice a little more calmness.
b. Learn to manage yourself.
c. Be responsible for your own emotional reactivity to challenging circumstances.

After three or four weeks of this effort, observe your growth. Are your relationships improving? Is your relationship with yourself better? Are you letting go of self-sabotage and replacing it with self-respect and confidence? These results will come as you practice. Your efforts will build your own maturity. Please share your success with me for inclusion in the follow-up book at connect@ibetherapy.com.

What this means on a broader basis

As you change yourself, the positive change in you becomes attractive to others. One sign is that people will smile at you more. This is the best kind of contagion—a spreading of emotional health, emotional maturity, emotional intelligence, smiles, and wisdom.

Through your continuing efforts to be a person of integrity, you will see others around you practicing higher principles more often, integrating their behavior with their conscience.

Their mature characters will also become appealing to others surrounding them. You will see the magnetic power of Bowen theory spreading beyond your own life. There will be no need to convince others to do what you are doing. Your example will be enough. Of course, if someone asks what you are doing, that person is receptive and wants to know—yet another positive sign.

By making a sincere effort to improve your own relationships and your life, you will find yourself witnessing a heartening societal progression from the ground level. You will have the satisfaction that you contributed.

As you age and mature, I wish you the pleasure and blessing of seeing the beauty of your character reflected in the beauty of character shining in the generations to come.

Appendix 1
How iBE Therapy was Developed

To help you to understand and use healthier relationship principles, this book explains key aspects of Bowen theory and EMDR. The explanations give you a more complete understanding of how and why the suggested approaches work. These two theories have been combined into iBE therapy to help you form healthier relationships and to heal your relationships that may be off track.

If you're reading this book, you may not be concerned about what theories or tools you are using to change your relationships. But if you are, you may want to understand in a bit more detail how iBE therapy draws from Bowen theory and EMDR.

When theories are combined to form new therapies, the approach is not always to use the whole of either theory, but to choose their most useful aspects and combine them into something new. For instance, many cancer patients today take the best of Western medicine and complementary approaches to achieve better results than either mode of practice achieves by itself.

With that understanding, the parts of Bowen theory I adapted into iBE therapy include Bowen's:

1. Clear and simple observations of the anxiety-binding mechanisms (ABMs) people use in response to their anxiety: conflict; distance and cutoff; triangling; and overfunctioning/underfunctioning reciprocity.
2. Description of emotional maturity and health, which I have adapted and called maturity-building principles: understanding, connection, direct commitment, and balance and equality. I also adapted variations of wise

conflict/differing; wise distance; wise triangling; and wise overfunctioning/underfunctioning reciprocity.

3. Guidance for clients to practice the calm neutrality of an interested observer or researcher in one's own family and to note the roles one plays in the family patterns.

4. Practice of coaching individuals to take full responsibility for the part they play in each relationship.

5. Vision of the broadest psychology approach from his time to the present. This includes his:

   a. Observation of how the patterns progress or regress across the generations.

   b. Understanding of each person as completely and as neutrally as possible.

      i. Avoidance of taking sides in emotional challenges.

      ii. Appreciation of the experience and view of each individual.

6. Emphasis on neutrality:

   a. To become more positive about individuals seen negatively by others,

   b. To find more balanced view of people perceived as family saints.

7. Decision to avoid diagnosis and instead focus on describing behavioral patterns in relationships.

8. Respect for the ability of humans to be able to learn, understand, and practice Bowen family systems theory.

9. Understanding that even the most emotionally-mature people do not always operate at their peak. Under enough stress, their functioning can decline. However, they will tend to make a quicker, more complete return to their usual mode of functioning. He predicted a less-mature person dealing with great stress may make a slower or even incomplete recovery. [I believe EMDR can change that result for even the less-mature person, because all humans have an AIP.]

10. Patient, positive view that even microscopic progress is huge.

The concepts of EMDR therapy I included in iBE therapy:

1. Francine Shapiro created and researched the clear, eight-phase protocol that can be researched and replicated. There have been 26 randomized control studies confirming the positive effects of EMDR. This has led the World Health Organization to recommend EMDR as one of only two recommended treatments for PTSD. She integrated client-centered, psycho-dynamic, cognitive behavioral, exposure, free association, mindfulness, body oriented, and interpersonal systems psychotherapies into a comprehensive therapy approach.
2. The assessment phase of EMDR accesses the visual image of the memory, the negative thought about self, the emotion that goes with the experience, and the location in the body where the emotion is felt. All four components of memory are equal in importance. Addressing the components together help the client to no longer react to the images, not believe the negative thoughts, not fear the emotions or remain controlled by them, and to positively observe their bodies relaxing.
3. Shapiro strongly encouraged trainees to integrate their EMDR practice into their existing specialties.
4. She created the information processing model, described that psychopathology arises from dysfunctionally-stored memories. With the help of EMDR calming and processing memories, they can then be functionally stored in the brain as the adaptive information processing (AIP) system (described in chapter 2) is activated. The newly coded information becomes available as resources in future.
5. She structured treatment into a three-pronged protocol: the first agenda for treatment is to address past memories of stress or trauma, the second is current triggers, and the final focus is positive future templates to facilitate adaptive future action.

6. The openness of Shapiro to adaptations of the therapy for specific populations or issues has resulted in a variety of researched applications for issues such as anxiety disorders (panic and phobia), obsessive-compulsive disorder, mood disorders, addictions, pain conditions, somatic conditions, couples and family therapy, and group therapy. It is due to the development of the EMDR group therapy protocol of Jarero that iBE now has the potential to help many people to affordably access comprehensive iBE treatment for complex relationship challenges.
7. The efficiency of EMDR is inherent in the standard protocol. The progress has been more rapid than considered possible for mental and emotional healing. As a field we accepted that mental healing was slow, and Bowen was no exception to this view. He was distrustful of "quick fixes." Though EMDR is not a quick fix, its efficiency, and its identification and activation of the Adaptive Information Processing system have changed the possibilities for humans.

iBE does not incorporate some aspects of Bowen theory. These include:

1. Bowen's avoidance of emotions. The reason for this is that EMDR therapy helps people discover that emotions offer useful information. As EMDR calms the emotions, the inherent health and strength of the AIP system reinforces the individual's clarity about themselves.

   Additionally, an EMDR protocol by Katie O'Shea, called resetting the affective circuits, helps people understand the value of the emotions. She addresses two categories based in part on studies by Jaak Panksepp, who researched mammalian (animal) brains in an effort to understand human brains and emotions.

He described the emotions as vertical channels in the brain and referred to them as circuits:

   a.   Protective, life-preserving emotions such as healthy shame, compassion, disgust, fear, anger and rage, and panic/grief.
   b.   Life-enhancing, regenerating, connective E-motions such as pride, gratitude, curiosity and seeking, joy, love and lust, and caring. She calls it E-motion, because once the emotion is felt completely, it releases energy for appropriate action.

By stimulating different areas of the brain and studying them, Panksepp identified seven primary circuits (primal emotions) in all mammals. O'Shea believes humans have more. These areas can be identified, mapped, and shown in brain scans.

2.   Bowen's concern about fusing with clients and readers—in other words, the tendency to lose one's identity by identifying too closely with the therapist or coach. The reason for this omission is that with each EMDR session people are less suggestible to incorrect information. I believe this is due to AIP activation, which protects clients from fusion. I let clients know that their brain will be the star of this show. Clients discover and learn to trust their internal resources. They commonly tell me, "I feel more myself!" And as I mentioned earlier in the book, Beth said, "I feel more like myself, but a better version of myself." Though such clients can learn to trust the therapist, it is quite different from fusing with the therapist. EMDR clients trust themselves more and more. This is far more reinforcing than fusing with or overly depending upon a therapist.

3.   Bowen did not believe in the unconscious or in other hypothesized structures in the psyche unconfirmed by objective science. He preferred to avoid the word

unconscious and instead described habits as automatic. I use both words because many readers understand both. Both help convey the danger of operating based on habit without conscious thought or choice. Automatic, unconscious actions will weaken any effort at emotional maturity. I believe Bowen would agree with this even if he didn't use some of the same vocabulary.

I have not omitted any aspect of EMDR therapy from the iBE protocol. However, I have added significant education about Bowen theory to the phase 2 preparation phase of the EMDR protocol.

Appendix 2
Pop Quiz Key

Your pop quiz responses reflect your own sincere experiences. There are no absolute right or wrong answers but there are healthier answers to aim for as you apply Bowen theory to increase your emotional maturity. I will indicate the ideals when possible.

Please give yourself honest feedback. The goal is to think about your choices and notice there are often other options. Some options can bring greater satisfaction for you and your relationships.

Chapter 2
If you cannot answer according to the key below yet, you may decide to work toward desensitization.

F   I've been emotionally triggered by someone's words, decision, or behavior and couldn't get past it for some time.

T   I have the kind of sensitivity that allows me to feel compassionate and considerate of the feelings and needs of others.

F   I often become so emotional I cannot think or reason clearly.

F   I tend to get hurt and withdraw from people without warning.

F   I don't like to think about how challenging it is for others to be close to me.

Chapter 3
Ideal behavior minimizes the harm caused to others by any urges toward conflict, criticism, or control. Regarding the third item, the ideal is to have self-control rather than being controlled by others.

T or F   I have felt battered by cruel or critical words.

T or F   Others have been forceful with me physically and I don't like it.

T or F   I really appreciate bossy and controlling people.

T or F   Conflict has caused me to leave a relationship (T/F), a job (T/F), a school (T/F).

T or F   I was completely blamed for a problem by a family member. It still bothers me.

Chapter 4

T   I have experienced the deep satisfaction of understanding someone in a new way.

T   I've put my own feelings aside to listen to another person.

T   Even if feeling upset, I've hung in there with a difficult conversation.

T   I've overcome conflict with someone and the relationship has improved.

T   I've experienced that blame and criticism are less satisfying than understanding.

Chapter 5

F   I live in a bubble that keeps me separate from people with differing views.

F   When I am uncomfortable with someone's behavior or speech, I withdraw.

F   Distance and avoidance are my safe places.

F   I have broken off relationships suddenly without allowing any discussion.

T or F   I've experienced pain when someone has cut off from me. It still bothers me.

Chapter 6

T   I have reconnected with and forgiven someone whom I wrote off for a time.

F   When I cut off from someone, they don't exist anymore.

T   When I move to a new location, I maintain close relationships despite the miles.

F   I find it hard to share what is really going on with me emotionally.

T   When someone cuts off abruptly from me, I work patiently to repair our connection.

Chapter 7

All these items are forms of triangling. The ideal is to manage one's own anxiety until calm enough to practice maturity-building mechanisms instead of anxiety-binding mechanism. In this way you will not pass on any anxiety and/or pain to others.

T or F I have witnessed gossip or experienced being the target of put-downs, untruths, and cruel words by more than one person.

T or F I've been betrayed romantically.

T or F My parents worry about me a lot at certain times in my life.

T or F I find myself thinking about my own children more than I do about my spouse.

T or F When I'm angry with someone, I'm likely to let others know all about it.

Chapter 8

The first and last items have a definite most healthy position. The other items are personal, based on experience. It is good to become conscious of what you have been doing, and to offer yourself fresh choices based on what you are learning here.

T   I am worthy of committed relationships.

T or F I am afraid to commit in a relationship due to all the bad relationships I've seen.

T or F I can see how I volunteer to be the center of attention, and how it hurts me sooner or later.

T or F I can see ways I was influenced to believe that making children number one is ideal.

T   When someone gossiped, I have said, "I don't want to gossip. Let's change the subject."

Chapter 9

Though these refer to personal experience, the locus of control is in the individual rather than with experiences controlled by others. Hence, I am indicating ideal answers.

F   I sometimes ask for help habitually, though I may not have needed it.

F   I'm quite certain I know what is best for certain other people.

T   I am responsible for my own happiness. I don't give others that responsibility.

F   I tend to jump "all in" to any challenge. Others take advantage of that and slack off.

F   I find it hard to choose goals and stick to them.

Chapter 10

Though these refer to personal experience, it is healthiest to place the locus of control in yourself rather than with experiences controlled by others. Hence, I am indicating ideal answers.

T   I can identify three relationships in which I enjoy an equal give and take.

T   I am annoyed by a friend who only talks and doesn't take time to listen to me.

F   I sometimes find myself hiding my behavior from others.

F   I get more attention for my overdoing than anything else in life.

F   I can't stand being stressed or pressured and prefer to take it easy most of the time.

Chapter 11

F   I have noticed that I act differently depending upon who I am with.

T   I can think of three things I respect about myself.

T   Even when stressed I can maintain calm and balance in my life.

F   I can't let it go when I run into roadblocks in my life.

T   My decisions take into account my feelings and
        thoughts but are not determined by my emotions or the
        demands of others.

Appendix 3
The Golden Rule

The principle of the golden rule is a perfect universal guide for emotional maturity. It can be found in many religions and philosophies. Isn't it inspiring that this wide variety of belief systems from East and West are saying the same thing?

Christianity
So, in everything, do to others what you would have them do to you, for this sums up the Law and the Prophets. Matthew 7:12

Sikhism
I am a stranger to no one; and no one is a stranger to me. Indeed, I am a friend to all. Guru Granth Sahib, p. 1299

Confucianism
One word sums up the basis of all good conduct: loving kindness. Do not do to others what you would not want done to yourself. Confucius, Analects 15:23

Buddhism
Treat not others in ways that you yourself would find hurtful. The Buddha, Udana-Varga 5.18

Hinduism
This is the sum of the Dharma (duty): do naught to others which would cause pain if done to you.

Baha'i Faith
Lay not on any soul a load that you would not wish to be laid upon you, and desire not for anyone the things you would not desire for yourself. Baha'u'llah, Gleanings.

Islam
Not one of you truly believes until you wish for others what you wish for yourself. The Prophet Muhammad, Hadith

Judaism
What is hateful to you, do not do to your neighbor. Tis is the whole Torah' all the rest is commentary. Go and learn it. Hillel, Talmad, Shabbat 31a

Jainism
One should treat all creatures in the world as one would like to be treated. Mavira, Sutrakritanga 1.11.33

Native Spirituality
We are as much alive as we keep the earth alive. Chief Dan George

Unitarianism
We affirm and promote respect for the interdependent web of all existence of which we are a part. Unitarian principle

Bibliography

Andrews, Andy. *The Traveler's Gift: Seven Decisions that Determine Personal Success.* Nashville: Thomas Nelson, 2002.

Ashton, Marvin J., "The Tongue Can Be a Sharp Sword" Speech, April 1992 General Conference of The Church of Jesus Christ of Latter Day Saints.

Bregman, Ona Cohn and Charles M. White. *Bringing Systems Thinking to Life.* London: Routledge, 2011.

Bowen, Murray. *Family Therapy in Clinical Practice.* Lantham, MD: Jason Aronson, 1978.

Bowen, Murray and Michael Kerr. *Family Evaluation.* New York City: W.W. Norton & Company, 1988.

Brown, Brene. *Rising Strong.* New York City: Spiegel and Grau, 2015.

Brown, Jenny. "Bowen Family systems Theory and Practice: Illustration and Critique." *Australian and New Zealand Journal of Family Therapy* 20, no. 2 (1999), 94-103.

Brown, Jenny. *Growing Yourself Up: How to Bring Your Best to All of Life's Relationships.* Wollumbi, NSW, Australia: Exisle Publishing, 2012.

Cohen-Posey, Kate. *Making Hostile Words Harmless.* Hoboken, NJ: John Wiley & Sons, Inc., 2008.

Early, Jay and Bonnie Weiss. *Freedom from Your Inner Critic.* Louisville, CO: Sounds True, 2013.

Epstein, Lewis. *Coaching for Fatherhood–Teaching Men New Life Roles.* Liberty Corner, NJ: New Horizon Press, 1996.

Epstein, Lewis. *More Coaching for Fatherhood.* Liberty Corner, NJ: New Horizon Press, 2008.

Feinberg, M., R. Willer, J. Stellar, D. Keitner. "The Virtues of Gossip: Reputational Information Sharing as Prosocial Behavior." *Journal of Personality and Social Psychology* 201: no.5 (2012)*: 1015-30, Epub 2012 Jan 9.*

Felitti, Vincent, et al., "Relationship of Childhood Abuse and Household Dysfunction to Many of the Leading Causes of

Death in Adults." *American Journal of Preventive Medicine* 14, no. 4 (May 1998): 245-258.

Fenton, Kevin. "How healthy behavior supports children's wellbeing." *Public Health England* August 28, 2013. PHE publications gateway number: 2013146 https://www.gov.uk/government/publications/how-healthy-behaviour-supports-childrens-wellbeing.

Gilbert, Roberta M. *Connecting with Our Children.* Hoboken, NJ: John Wiley & Sons, 1999.

Gilbert, Roberta M. *The Eight Concepts of Bowen Theory.* Lake Frederick, VA: Leading Systems Press, 2004, 2006.

Gilbert, Roberta M. *Extraordinary Relationships.* Minneapolis, MN: Chronimed Publishing, 1992.

Gomez, Ana M. *Dark, Bad Day...Go Away!* Phoenix, AZ: Ana M. Gomez Publisher, 2007.

Haidt, Jonathan. "Can a divided America heal?" November 2016 TED Talk.

The International Council of 13 Indigenous Grandmothers. *For the Next 7 Generations.* Documentary. Directed by Bruce Hart and Carol Hart. 2009. Beyond Words Distributor, DVD. http://www.grandmotherscouncil.org/for-the-next-7-generations-the-movie.

Jarero, Ignacio, Artigas, Lucina, Hartung, John. "EMDR Integrative Group Treatment Protocol: A Postdisaster Trauma Intervention for Children and Adults." *Traumatology,* 12(2), 121-129, June 1, 2006. https://doi.org/10.1177/1534765606294561.

Kabatznick, Ronna and Margaret Cullen, "The Traveling Peacemaker: A Conversation with Marshall Rosenberg" *Inquiring Mind,* Fall 2004. http://www.inquiringmind.com/Articles/Peacemaker.html.

Keen, Sam. *Fire in the Belly: On Being a Man.* London: Bantam, 1991.

Kerr, Michael E. and Bowen, Murray. *Family Evaluation—An Approach Based on Bowen Theory.* New York City: W. W. Norton & Company, Inc., 1988.

Kerr, Michael E. *One Family's Story: A Primer on Bowen Theory*. Washington, DC: Bowen Center for the Study of the Family, 2002.

Krouse Rosenthal, Amy, "You May Want to Marry My Husband" *The New York Times,* March 3, 2017 https://www.nytimes.com/2017/03/03/style/modern-love-you-may-want-to-marry-my-husband.html.

Lathrap, Mary T. "Judge Softly." Publisher unknown, 1895.

Lincoln, Abraham. August 1, 1858. Written and signed in the form of an autograph, from *The Wit and Wisdom of Abraham Lincoln* edited by H. Jack Lang. Cleveland, New York City: World Publishing Company 1943, 1965.

Maloney-Scharer, Andrea, "AIDS and the Family," *Family Center Report* 10: no. 1, Georgetown Family Center, 1989.

Maloney-Scharer, Andrea, "The Family Emotional Unit and Responses to HIV/AIDS." Paper selected for presentation by the Office on AIDS at NAMH, Second Annual Meeting, 1994.

Mandela, Nelson. *Long Walk to Freedom: The Autobiography of Nelson Mandela*. New York City: Little, Brown and Company, 1994.

Mandela, Nelson. *The Long Walk to Freedom*. Directed by Justin Chadwick. 2013. Paris: Pathé, 2014. DVD.

Medicine Crow, Joe. "Joseph Medicine Crow, Completed All Requirements to Become the Last Crow War Chief in WWII." March 3, 2016. https://www.warhistoryonline.com.

Miller, Robert, "The Feeling-State Theory of Impulse-Control Disorders and the Impulse-Control Disorder Protocol" *Traumatology* 16: no. 3 (2010): 2-10.

Miller, Robert, "Treatment of Behavioral Addictions Utilizing the Feeling-State Addictions Protocol: A Multiple Baseline Study" *Journal of EMDR Practice and Research* 6: no. 4 (2012): 50-59.

Miller, Robert, Advanced EMDR Training in Feeling-State Addiction Protocol, presented 2012, San Diego, CA.

O'Shea, Katie, M.S. and Paulsen, Sandra, PhD. "Resetting the Affective Circuits" *When There are No Words: EMDR for Early Trauma and Neglect Held in Implicit Memory.*

Panksepp, J. "The science of emotions: Jaak Panksepp" TED Talk, Jan. 13, 2014.

Papero, Daniel, "Managing Self in a Fearful World," presentation, March 18, 2017, San Diego, CA.

Rosenberg, Marshall. (2015, Third Edition. 2003, Second Edition) *Non-violent Communication: A Language of Life,* PuddleDancer Press *(*1999, First Edition*) Nonviolent Communication: A Language of Compassion,* Encinitas, CA: PuddleDancer Press.

Rosenberg, Ross. *The Human Magnet Syndrome.* Brecksville, OH: CMI Education Institute, 2013.

Rudolph, Wilma. *Wilma: The Story of Wilma Rudolph.* New York City: Signet, 1977.

Scott, M.J. and S.G. Stradling. "Post-traumatic stress disorder without the trauma." *Brit J Clin Psychol* 33 (Feb. 1994): 71-4.

Shapiro, Francine. "Efficacy of the eye movement desensitization procedure in the treatment of traumatic memories." *Journal of Traumatic Stress, 2*: 199-223, 1989a.

Shapiro, Francine. "Eye movement desensitization: A new treatment for post-traumatic stress disorder." *Journal of Behavior Therapy and Experimental Psychiatry, 20*: 211-217, 1989b.

Shapiro, Francine. *Getting Past Your Past: Take Control of Your Life with Self-Help Techniques from EMDR Therapy.* New York: Rodale, 2012.

Shapiro, Francine. *Eye Movement Desensitization and Reprocessing (EMDR) Therapy: Basic Principles, Protocols, and Procedures.* New York: Guilford Press, Third Edition, 2017.

Siegel, Robert. 2017. "All Things Considered." *National Public Radio,* May 12, 2017.

Skowron, Elizabeth and Myrna Friedlander. "The Differentiation of Self Inventory: Development and Initial Validation." *Journal of Counseling Psychology,* 45(3), 235-246, 1998.

Stone, H. and Stone. Embracing Your Inner Critic: Turning Self-Criticism into a Creative Asset. Harper San Francisco, 1993.

Stickgold, R. "EMDR: A putative neurobiological mechanism of action." *J. Clin. Psychology* 58 (2002): 61–75. doi:10.1002/jclp.1129.

Teicher, MH, JA Samson, YS Sheu, A Polcari, CE McGreenery. "Hurtful words: association of exposure to peer verbal abuse with elevated psychiatric symptom scores and corpus callosum abnormalities." *American Journal of Psychiatry,* 167(12), 1464-71, DEC 2010. doi: 10.1176/appi.ajp.2010.10010030. Epub 2010 Jul 15.

Titelman, Peter, ed. *Emotional Cutoff.* Philadelphia: The Haworth Clinical Practice Press, 2003.

Titelman, Peter, ed. *Triangles Bowen Family Systems Theory Perspectives.* New York City: The Haworth Press, 2008.

van der Koch, Bessel, J. Spinazzola, ME Blaustein, JW Hopper, DL Korn, WB Simpson. "A randomized clinical trial of eye movement desensitization and reprocessing (EMDR), fluoxetine, and pill placebo in the treatment of posttraumatic stress disorder." *Journal of Clinical Psychiatry,* 68(1), 37-46, Jan. 2007.

Woodward, Cheryl Anne. (copyright 2017) Personal correspondence. All rights reserved, with use permission granted to Dana Terrell.

West, Cornel and Bell Hooks. *Breaking Bread: Insurgent Black Intellectual Life.* Brooklyn, New York: South End Press, 1991.

Index

A

ABMs (anxiety-binding mechanisms)
 as automatic and hidden, 10, 12,
  92, 201, 204, 212, 259
 as destructive in long-term, 181,
  202, 204, 244, 259
 as habits or addictions, 90, 101,
  104, 128, 137, 205
 as rewarding in short-term, 101,
  181, 202, 204, 212, 244, 259
 as skills, 169–70
 Bowen's research on, 24–25, 83,
  170, 259
 consciousness of, 201, 204, 212,
  229, 259
 definition of, 83
 examples of, 170, 185
 iBE therapy and, 10
 in combination, 199, 259
 intergenerational transmission
  of, 181, 196
 list of four patterns, 24–25, 91
 maturity-building principles
  (MBPs) as replacements for,
  12, 25, 171, 212, 259, 260,
  271
 shifting targets of, 189–90
 therapeutic analysis of, 216–18
 vs. wise protective patterns, 92,
  93
 See also conflict; distance in
  relationships; one up/one
  down reciprocity; triangling
adaptive information processing
 (AIP). See AIP (adaptive
 information processing) systems

addictions
 ABMs as, 101, 205

codependent relationships and,
 204, 205
feeling-state addiction protocol
 (FSAP), 205
in one up/one down reciprocity,
 201, 205–6, 219
with pain meds, 207–8
Adverse Childhood Experiences
 Survey (ACES), 79, 86, 105
affairs (love triangles), 156–59, 175,
 178, 185–88
aggressiveness. See conflict
ahisma (nonviolence) principle, 83,
 90
AIDS patients, research on, 142–43
AIP (adaptive information
 processing) systems
 activation of, 55, 63, 258
 and positive sensitivity, 69–70
 as healer of anxiety, 259
 case studies of, 62–65, 65, 71,
  74–76, 218
 definition of, 39, 52–53
 desensitization and, 54, 55, 81
 emotional overload and, 54, 64
 exercises for activation of, 65–69
All Things Considered (Siegel), 94–95
Amen, Daniel, 60–61
American Psychiatric Association, 73
Anderson, Kip, 34
Andrews, Andy, 177
Anthony, Susan B., 235–36
anxieties
 acceptance of, 49
 and intergenerational
  transmission, 181, 196
 as cause of conflict, 89
anxieties *(continued)*
 Bowen theory for, 49, 79–80, 80
 EMDR therapy for, 49, 79–80, 80

CPSIA information can be obtained
at www.ICGtesting.com
Printed in the USA
FSHW01n1837040618
48770FS